anna

A life of stubbornness made into joyous service

anna

A life of stubbornness made into joyous service

by
Betty Barkman

Kindred Press

Winnipeg, Manitoba, Canada   Hillsboro, Kansas, U.S.A.

Anna.

All Scripture quotations are taken from the King James Bible.

All quotations of songs and poems, where the source is known, are used by permission.

Published simultaneously by Kindred Press, 4-169 Riverton Avenue, Winnipeg, MB R2L 2E5 and 315 S. Lincoln Street, Hillsboro, KS 67063.

Printed in Canada by The Christian Press, Winnipeg.

International Standard Book Number: 0-919797-10-5

PREFACE

Heroes are people like you and me — not extraordinary super men and women. They are people who have been "made strong in weakness." This strength has given them the power to fight valiantly so that enemies have fled in terror. Because of their faith in God, they have subdued kingdoms, brought about righteousness, received promises and escaped the edge of the lance, but they have also suffered illness, endured hardship and survived persecution. The writer of Hebrews refers to them as people "of whom the world was not worthy."

This book is about one such person and her circle of loved ones. Let me tell you how it came about.

As I stepped into the foyer at the back of our little country church where my husband is the pastor, I saw her. I observed nothing noticeable different about her and yet it seemed she carried a glow. Something nudged me, saying, "There is one of God's special servants," but I chided myself, thinking, "That's silly! Aren't we all God's chosen ones?"

Anna and John had come to our church to share and present their Bolivian missionary experience. The service, poorly attended, was nice but nothing glamorous or extraordinary happened. At the end my husband prodded me, "There *is* something here. Make sure you get to know that woman. Invite them over for coffee."

I had never seen the couple before, and knew nothing about them or their family, nothing about their past or background, or even their nationality. Their name sounded Mennonite, but I was convinced that she, perhaps because of her dark hair and foreign accent, must be of Spanish-Indian background.

After the hour fellowship at our house, I knew I had experienced something special. An unforgettable friendship was begun. But, I was completely unprepared for my husband's comments as we prepared for bed.

"You must write Anna's story." he said with conviction.

"No way!" I retorted. "In the first place there isn't enough material, and in the second place I couldn't sell it. The world isn't interested in such stories."

A few days later he approached me again. My retort was not quite as vehement. After his third try to convince me, I was convicted of rebellion and agreed to pray about it. Almost immediately I felt the Spirit moving me to a more positive attitude. Perhaps I had been wrong. It seemed impossible, but at least I would consider it.

Finally I put myself out on a limb and phoned Anna. I popped the question bluntly, taking her totally by surprise. Would she be interested in sharing her story with me, right down to the nitty-gritty, and let me publish it for everyone to read? I didn't know her story, I only knew she had one.

She agreed to pray about it and discuss it with her husband and family. Several days later she returned the call. "Your proposal makes me feel very small and unworthy. Yet the more we've prayed about it, the more convinced we've become. God wants me to open up and share my story with the world. But only for His honor, not for my own."

Thus began a chain of events and long hours of work. It meant many interviews with Anna and getting to know her family. It meant many 60 kilometer drives to her house in our rickety old car. It meant having a Kleenex box handy as I wept with her in reliving pains of the past and again as we rejoiced together about each new victory.

For me it rapidly became a very enriching experience, but for my family it meant patience and acceptance. Each one demonstrated whole-hearted support, even though my husband occasionally wondered — had he made the right suggestion after all? It took so much of my time and effort.

Many thanks to our daughters, Jolyn and Laurie who

helped with the typing and proof reading. This was a bigger help than they knew.

Thank you also to Esther Wiens, Mennonite Brethren Bible College, Winnipeg, who gave very worthwhile assistance. It was greatly appreciated.

Finally, a big thank you to Martha Kroeker, who retyped the final manuscript for submission to the publisher.

After having worked through Anna's story, I know I can never be the same again. The glow that radiates from someone like Anna is so brilliant, it sets others aglow. May you too, be inspired and changed as you read *Anna.*

Betty Barkman
Pansy, Manitoba

INTRODUCTION

I first saw John and Anna Wiens in the kitchen of the New Tribes school in Tambo, Bolivia. They were new there and looked young and vulnerable. Yet there was an intangible something about both that drew me. I wanted to get to know them. But a language barrier and my own busy-ness got in the way.

Now, many years later Betty Barkman's story has fallen into my hands and I am profoundly grateful to learn the whole tale. I had not realized that Betty was writing about someone I knew, or about areas and events in the heart of South America with which I was familiar, so that I was hooked before I realized it.

I would have been hooked anyway. Anna's story is told perceptively, without sentimentality and with a grasp of the issues involved. I grew angrier the longer I read — angry that only the few, like Anna and John, face the pains and the cost of truly following Christ. For the rest of us Christianity is a pleasant hobby. Anna and John grappled with the powers of Hell, and suffered as Christ suffered — indeed as all of us would suffer if we were to follow as they do.

I was angry, but I was also heartened and renewed. If there are those who play at Christianity, there are also those who, whether at home or in deserts, urban slums or jungles, count all things but loss for the glory of following Christ into battle. For as Anna discovered, it was not primarily her sacrificial service God wanted (and her service was nothing if not sacrificial) but her self, that he might share *himself* with her, as she shared life with him.

My prayer is that Betty Barkman's book will create a thirst in its readers to discover for themselves Anna's secret glory.

Dr. John White
Author, lecturer and former U of M Professor
Kenora, Ontario

x

Chapter one

DARKNESS hung heavily that night in the plain little mud brick cabin. Anna eased herself ever so gently back into the squeaky high-poster bed. It wouldn't do to awaken Abe. He needed his rest.

Waves of weariness threatened to engulf her, as she snuggled under her bit of blanket and wished for oblivion. She needed sleep, real sleep, sleep that could keep her from hearing the ever-recurring screams of her baby at the other end of the room.

"Oh no," Anna thought wearily "is that the baby again?" She shuddered involuntarily as she thought about the restless turning of that tiny bit of humanity. Any minute now she expected to hear the heartbreaking outcry of pain — pain that she couldn't understand. Anna felt helpless. Was it worth the effort to blow out the lantern and try to get some sleep?

At 22, Anna, in the privacy of her own room under the supervision of a midwife, had given birth to her third child. Baby Anna, however, had not arrived as third. She was in fact, like the long awaited first born, a special treasure. The two previous attempts to begin a family had ended in failure and heartbreak. Both infants had lived pitifully short lives. The first, born prematurely, never had a chance, and the second, in a state of awful convulsions, had died when he was less than three weeks old.

The movements and noises in the cradle were increasing. Anna finally rose to pick up the baby, wanting to calm her before the screams became too piercing. Gently she held the baby, caressing, cuddling, stroking its back; anything that could possibly relieve the pain that was upsetting it. "If only I knew what was the matter," she mused. "If only I knew of someone who could help."

1

The sounds of the sick baby persisted and soon began to mingle with her own smothered sobs. Her tears fell unheeded on the soft little mussed up blanket. Then the thought of God came to her. Hadn't she always believed? Hadn't she always prayed? Her other prayers hadn't been answered, at least not visibly, but maybe if she prayed like never before, maybe . . . maybe God was her answer.

Praying aloud was traditional taboo, and not to be considered. She knew no praying forms or rules, but she knew that she must pray. And pray she would! Hesitantly, in the soul-whispers that she was most familiar with, she began. She'd rock and stroke the baby, and breathe a prayer. Rock, cuddle and pat the now whimpering baby, and breathe more prayers.

"Oh God," came the cry from her hurting heart, "You know how I want this baby, how I need it! I wanted my other babies too, but You wanted them more and so You took them. You have them now. But please let me keep this one. Please don't let her die, God!"

She stopped to swallow a sob, and yearningly looked at the bundle in her arms, at the coal black hair, the long dark lashes over brown eyes that would grow to be pretty. With a sigh, she continued. "You know how I love her. She . . . she seems so . . . so like she should, like she should live. But I don't know what is wrong with her. Can You show me what to do, dear God, or can you simply heal her with Your touch?"

There was a pause. Finally she burst out, "I don't know what to pray, or how, but show me, God, *please show me!* Please God!"

Gradually the restlessness in Anna's heart left. She noticed with joy that the baby had fallen soundly asleep in her arms. Gently Anna settled the baby back into the cradle, and in the dim light of the flickering little lamp, she saw a peaceful half-smile cross the baby's face and linger there. Deeply moved, Anna whispered, "Thank you, God. You are real! You heard my prayer."

That was the turning point. The hours of screaming got shorter and fewer, and Anna felt in her heart that God was close and real. Surely He loved her and had some sort of purpose for her. It struck her that He might like some response from her. Had He not heard the cry of her heart in the darkest night? She remembered Hannah and thought, "I will give my baby back to God too, if He will let her live and be healed of her trouble." Then, although she didn't tell anyone or even say the words aloud, she made it a secret little vow, a vow she could never quite forget throughout the coming years.

"This baby is God's baby. She is someone that God made and wants for His glory, somewhere, somehow." That thought imprinted itself strongly on Anna's mind, and remained there.

Anna had reason to hang on to her trust in God. There was little else! Human resources and wisdom, according to her experience, equalled little more than nothing.

It was 1940, and only some thirteen years after a large group of her people — Mennonites by faith and Dutch by nationality, had emigrated from Canada, and settled in what was then the totally unfamiliar and poverty-stricken country of Paraguay. Anna's family, like most of its neighbors, maintained Canadian citizenship, but that fact did not bring them many privileges. Living in Loma Plata, in the heart of the Chaco in western Paraguay, was perhaps reason enough to lift up one's eyes to a power higher than mere human. There were no doctors or hospitals for many miles around, and no vehicles to take a person to a place where there might be some. The home remedies that were used — local chiropractors, midwives, and other experts — were not based on any training or education. Books, which could have helped, were also hard to come by.

But little Anna slowly overcame, or outgrew, her problem and became a beautiful baby. When Anna was a few months old, the pain recurred, but now she was old enough to show and tell. With clenched fists, she rubbed her ears in rhythm with the screaming cries. Now her mother knew. Why hadn't anyone thought of it before? The baby had terrible ear infections.

Papa blew warm smoke into her ears; first once, then many times. The remedy helped. Even the expected hearing impairment never happened.

Anna grew, and became a robust, happy, energetic girl — the apple of her papa's eye. Some years later, as Anna watched little Anna and her papa go off to the fields together, hand in hand, she couldn't help but sigh. She turned back to her little brood in the house. The years had been good to her. Their family now included three brothers and six sisters for young Anna. What a joy to have such a nice, large family. But whenever she really thought about Anna, she remembered those awful, dark nights when the screams of the baby seemed never to end. She remembered that special night when she had prayed so earnestly. God had answered! The touch she felt from God that day had lingered long.

But, even now as she watched her Anna, so happy and energetic, she had unidentifiable sensations. What was this feeling she had about little Anna? Was God going to do special things for her, or use her in some specific way? Anna Sr. could not know. She could not even talk about such things. People would not understand. She did not even know if others cared. But God cared, this she knew! She could talk to Him in the secret of her heart, where no one could eavesdrop.

God's comfort filled her as she returned to her many duties. "Someday, perhaps soon, we will see God's reasons for all these things," she mused.

Chapter Two

NINE-YEAR-OLD Anna jumped up and down with excitement when Papa told the family the good news at the supper table. The Co-op, an official organization and the strength of the community, had succeeded in buying a large tract of land from the government. The new community would be Schoenau, located at Leg. 63, some 130 kilometers south of Loma Plata. "And," said Papa, "we will be among the very first to move. In fact, we need to get ready at once and move as soon as we can."

Moving meant preparation and bustling activity. Every possession worth keeping had to be prepared and packed for the long trail ride, and then placed appropriately in the old wooden wagon. What a lot of packing and repacking until everything fit in snugly. The horses were groomed and curried, their feet shod. Extra feed was prepared for the trip. The fact that Mama had no time or material to sew new clothes didn't matter. She and each of the children had at least one outfit to wear. Some had two or three so they could change, and the baby had several diapers. Was this not all they needed? Did they not have enough to be content and happy?

Anna had never heard of people owning large wardrobes and travelling with suitcases full of personal effects. She wouldn't have known what to do with so many clothes! But, Anna was careful to pack her own rag doll! The one Mama had made for Christmas a few years back. It definitely had to come along, even if she might not have time to play with it.

Right now she was busy, very busy! Between Mama's and Papa's commands, she couldn't decide whose errands were more important. But somehow she would get everything done! The excitement of it all, and her feeling of importance as the eldest helper, made Anna stand a little taller and run a little faster. Her dark brown eyes sparkled through most of her waking hours as she hurried from task to task.

Moving day came at last! Midst some cheerful goodbyes and just a few tears on Mama's eyelids that no one was supposed to see, the family set off. Soon though, too soon, the trip ahead began to smack of monotony. After all the excitement, the trip, to Anna seemed suddenly long and boring. She could only walk along behind the wagon train, or sit beside Mama and help with the little ones.

"I wish I had something to do," Anna grumbled aloud, as Mama looked knowingly at her. "Is there nothing we can do? Can we not go faster?"

The heat became oppressive. One day the dry reddish dust seemed especially eager to swirl all around them. Soon it covered the whole family with an even layer over their clothes, hair and skin. Everywhere, dust was clinging to their sticky sweaty bodies. Tiny rivulets of sweat trickled down their backs and faces, each forming a clean groove through the layer of dirt.

The picture suddenly looked most amusing to Anna. She couldn't help laughing, as she continued to look from one to the other. "We look like zebras! Only our stripes are going the wrong way, and . . . and maybe our color is wrong!"

Such moments of excitement helped relieve Anna's boredom, but they came too infrequently. When Anna thought she couldn't stand another hour of travelling, she snuggled up beside Papa. Was he still happy and enthusiastic? She couldn't quite tell. He looked very tired, about as tired as she felt.

"When will we *ever* get there?" she finally dared ask.

Papa looked tenderly at her, and sighed, "We're almost there. *Almost.*"

"There it is! Just beyond those trees."

He sounded and looked more eager now. Anna could tell as she watched his face. As each of the final kilometers rolled by, his weariness lifted some more. He began to whistle. Then he flashed Anna a rare grin which seemed to tell her a whole story.

"We're starting a new adventure, a whole new life. And you and I will be partners in it."

Her heart glowed with anticipation.

The portion of land allotted to the Giesbrecht family became not only their pride and joy, but very soon began developing into a bustling little cotton farm. It was their chance, the chance of a lifetime. Imagine, to settle on their own land and establish a farm that would hopefully let them go places.

Settling in was an adventure, although it meant living in a small shanty for the first little while, but when it came to the long days of hard physical labor, Anna wasn't so sure about this adventure. Loving her Papa as she did, she enjoyed the feeling of importance that came with the knowledge that she was fast becoming his most trusted right hand. Many days she was at his side from sun-up till sun-down, out in the sun and sweat, while the younger children stayed around the house to help Mama.

While Mama brewed a pot of coffee and was putting faspa on the table for their mid-afternoon break, Anna's well-tanned bare feet seemed restless under the brown wooden table. With her big toe she drew and re-drew the line along the bottom edge of the table leg. Her index finger found the worn-out corner of the checkered oil cloth cover and began pecking at it until the size of the hole began growing noticeably.

"Stop that!" Mama fairly hissed, more upset than was common for her.

Papa stepped into the makeshift kitchen just in time to hear the hasty command. "What happened?" he inquired of Mama.

Mama's explanation was quick and ready. *"That daughter of ours!* I can't understand it. When she works outside with you all day I feel sorry for her, but as soon as she gets a break, instead of enjoying it, she's restless and fidgety and . . . and *naughty!* She always has to have something to do!"

Half afraid, Anna looked up to see what Papa's reaction was. His disciplining hand was one thing she wasn't about to fool with, although lately she'd almost forgotten that. They were such good friends. A good look at his face now let her breathe easier. Behind the rather stern exterior, she saw just a hint of laughter, or so she thought. He said nothing, absolutely nothing. Was that supposed to mean that he forgave her, or would she be in trouble later?

After a quieter than usual snack, Papa pushed back his chair and cleared his throat. "You may come with me to the barn, Anna."

"Wow! Now I'll get it," she exclaimed to herself.

But papa was continuing. "I think it's time you learn to milk a cow."

"Oh, yea!" She wanted to shout it, but good girls aren't noisy, something told her. She sighed with relief, remained quiet, and hoped he hadn't read her mind.

And so began Anna's first milking lessons. Papa had purchased several cows and was hoping to build up a fine little herd. Surely a child that was going on ten was old enough to help.

Mostly the milking was in the mornings. During evening chores the young calves were allowed back to their mothers for a quickly devoured supper, a sight Anna never tired of watching.

When Anna understood that Papa was serious about teaching her to milk, she went at it with a will. She was anxious to prove herself, and rapidly became more proficient, although not without some hurts and tumbles.

At first her little fingers just didn't have enough strength, it seemed, to squeeze out that stubborn milk. When finally she succeeded and milked a whole cow on her own, her hands and arms were so tired and aching, she thought she'd die. She couldn't stand it! Even her knees were shaking!

The cows were not in proper stalls, but only tied up loosely for milking. One day — her fingernails may have been too long or perhaps the cow had a sore on its teat — Anna had barely begun milking when the cow jumped as if it had been pinched. Anna went sprawling! Her little bench fairly flew! The tin milking pail tumbled on its side, spilling all its contents.

Disgustedly Anna picked herself up and brushed off the dirt. Papa came running to check if she were hurt, but Anna only kept muttering, "That stupid cow," while bravely trying to forbid a few threatening tears.

Seeing that Anna was not hurt Papa made her go back to finish the job. He did stay right beside her, though, as if to make sure it wouldn't happen again.

By the time Anna was eleven, she regularly milked from four to eight cows every morning.

The main crop raised for the cattle's feed was cafer corn. The large huskless ears presented a problem, however, during the last several weeks before harvest. Like a magnet, they attracted parrots, doves and other corn-loving birds, all of whom seemed intent upon gathering the spoils before the harvest.

Papa came up with the perfect solution. His shrill whistle brought Anna to his side at once. "I've figured out what we must do. You get Daisy, ride her all over the field, and chase all the birds away."

"The whole field, Papa?" she queried, thinking that the 15-acre field looked rather vast. "And how long do I keep it up?"

"Yes, the whole field. You start at once and stop only when the sun goes down," he answered decisively.

Anna loved horseback riding. What an opportunity to do what she enjoyed! And, Daisy was her favorite mare. Whether it was herding cattle or rounding them up, she and Daisy were always together. The only time she changed for a different horse was in foaling time.

Off she went to find Daisy. Up and down the rows, round

and round the field they rode. This job tested Anna's spirit and patience more than it tested her riding skill. Hour after endless hour. The sun pushed the temperatures up to 90° and 100°F. At last it was dismounting time, and the weary girl dropped to the ground in exhaustion.

The next day Anna was at it again, from sun-up till sundown, and the next and the next. Some days the sun beat down mercilessly until she thought she'd roast alive. How could it be so hot!

For four weeks, seven days a week, Anna stuck to the job. Would it never end? Then suddenly it was harvest! She was relieved of her 'endless' job, only to have it replaced by the tedious chores connected with the corn harvest. Everything was done by hand. But the change was a blessing.

School in Schoenau started in May and lasted through September. For Anna this was a wonderful time of year. She loved to learn! Her lively outgoing personality thrived on the chance to associate daily with friends of her own age. Wherever the action was, there Anna was sure to be.

Although formally school closed in September, it opened again for a few weeks just prior to Christmas. At this time each student would memorize one long poem for Christmas and another for New Year's Day. They would learn new songs and rehearse the familiar Christmas songs. The students sang their hearts out. Soon all the songs had been memorized.

And then it was Christmas! The special school was over, but all the stored-up poetry was eagerly recited for many a fond grandparent and parent at family gatherings.

For Anna, the long holidays from school were anything but holidays. In fact, the thought of vacationing never entered her mind.

The 25 or 30 acres of cotton which Papa owned needed constant attention. As soon as possible after the October rains, the plowing began. Because the ground was hard and heavy, two to four horses pulled a one-share plow, and they had a full load.

"Anna," Papa announced early one morning. "Today you will learn to plow. We will harness the two best horses, Fred and Ben, for you. I will take the other four."

"Do you think . . . do you think I can do it?" Anna falteringly wondered aloud. But Papa did not hear, he had already gone out. He had all the confidence in the world, it seemed.

"Steady now. You can do it." His strong voice carried comfort, as she struggled with the reins, trying desperately to control both horses as well as the plow. For Papa's sake, she better do her best! If he thought she could do it, she would have to prove that she could. But her arms already felt numb and achy. Would they last through the hours ahead? Or would she have to quit? What if her horses would start acting up or run away?

Just when thoughts of fright and loneliness began to overwhelm her, she saw out of the corner of her eyes — she couldn't really look, for she must keep her eyes on her furrow — that Papa was really quite close. Just a little to her right and a wee bit behind. She got the feeling that he was watching her, ready to help in any emergency. Was that what God was like?

She soon mastered the art of ploughing. During the spring of her twelfth year she was at the job from beginning to end, about ten to fifteen days. This turned out to be a precedent for the years ahead. Papa always saved the best horses for her.

After the plowing came the planting. This was Papa's special job. He used only one horse, seeding the cotton with a one-row planter. The rows were three to four feet apart.

The break between seed time and weeding time was not long. As soon as the plants were about two inches high, Papa got in there with the horse and one-row cultivator. Up and down, up and down the rows he'd go. Anna, who was always around to "help," soon caught on to the job too, and it wasn't long before she could add the cultivation art to her list of skills.

11

But the hand weeding was another story. Wow, did that try her patience and persevering power! When it was possible, several members of the family would work at it together. With hoe in hand, each would struggle along the rows, often in the overwhelming heat. Another gigantic task which needed undertaking was the thinning out of the cotton plants. As any knowledgeable adult could have told Anna, one acre after thinning held about thirty to sixty thousand plants. By the time the weeding was done once, it was time to start over. Some years it had to be done three times! Weeds had such sneaky ways of catching up, and the family certainly could not afford to neglect its cotton crop. It was the main, and almost only, source of income.

One morning Anna found herself on the cotton field alone. The sun soon was high and hot. She was sweaty, tired and more than a little bored. "One more row," she'd push herself. "One more row." Then it was one foot after another, one weed after another. Oh, would she ever get done?

"What's the use?" she groaned. "I'm taking a break." She leaned her weary frame on her hoe. As she looked around she suddenly felt her spirits lift. But it was different than anything she'd felt before; everything even looked different. The warm sunshine was really beautiful and so were the green leaves of the cotton plants, swaying ever so slightly in the gentle breeze. Why had she never noticed it before? The thought jolted her — there is Someone somewhere who made all this! She looked again at the even rows of beautiful greenery — Papa's cotton in the making. And then she lifted her eyes upward. Up there somewhere was God. A God who — what? "If only I could be an angel, up there with God," Anna thought. Mama sometimes talked about angels. If she were to become an angel would that help her know God?

Did God plan the things down here? Did He control them? Did He, perhaps even right now, see this cotton field, and did He see her here right now, just a lone little figure in the middle of a vast field? Did He? Anna shivered. The thought was uncanny. A feeling of deep awe and reverence overcame her, and her thoughts became a prayer.

"Lord God, if You are there, if You are real, please could I learn to know You? I'd like to find out what life is all about. I'd like to know the reasons why things happen. There are reasons, aren't there? And plans? Do You have plans for people? For people like . . . well, like me, a skinny little nobody? And how would You show these plans, so I'd know? . . . Don't You have some kind of system for people to find out what Your plans are? . . ."

She stopped suddenly! Her prayer must be wrong. Probably God listened only to His chosen few, and would not listen to her. Who the chosen few might be she had no way of telling. If only she knew God! Then she could tell if He cared about her enough to listen.

Enough of this! She better get back to work.

In spite of the unanswered questions, Anna now had a new lightness in her step, a new strength in her body and joy in her heart. She couldn't verbalize the feeling but deep inside her heart she knew. She knew without a doubt that she had just had a very real and precious encounter with Someone. That Someone had to be God. And she knew with clarity, too, that she had begun a search; a search to find out if it were possible that God had a plan for her, and that she might know that plan. Would God show her? Would there come a time in her life when she'd know?

With a sparkle in her eye and a bounce in her step Anna put the hoe away and hurried into the house for dinner, and a well deserved break.

Life was good. Even while young Anna worked so hard in the steaming hot Chaco, she sensed God's presence. The feeling of expectancy stayed with her.

Anna, like the rest of her family, watched for the blooming of their precious cotton plants. Finally a few opened. Then suddenly, new flowers were popping up all over the field. At first they would be white, then they became pink and blue, and finally they dried up and fell to the ground. The first

13

flowers bloomed at the bottom of the plant, and, as the process continued, the blooming would finally finish at the top. The search for cotton balls therefore started with diligent searches among the bottom leaves of the plant. Some six weeks after the flowers had dropped, Anna could see the first cotton balls forming.

Anna enjoyed watching the green, golf-ball sized boll doing its final thing — cracking in four or five straight lines from the tip down, splitting open to show its fluffed out cotton. These dried bolls, called burrs, gave the plant the appearance of having clusters of fluffy snowballs. It was at this stage that the cotton was harvested.

After all that waiting, harvest time, in the middle of February, was suddenly upon them. This time it wasn't just Anna and her Papa who got ready to work. It was the whole family. Even a five-year old was big enough to help. All the lard cans and milk pails of the household were collected. Mama had worked hard to prepare food ahead of time in order to be ready for the harvest. Now she was in the field, together with the youngsters, leading the way, showing them how to pick the cotton.

Only the bolls at the bottom of the plants had matured, but they couldn't wait for the rest before picking these. What if a rain came unexpectedly to spoil the ready burrs?

The family worked hard, moving down the long rows one at a time, collecting by hand the ready cotton bolls, filling the pails and emptying them into the large sacks Papa had prepared. *Each* sack was filled carefully, as full as possible. *Each* ripened burr was gathered conscientiously, even the would-be strays. Was this not their livelihood? Their only chance ever to get ahead? After the bottom bolls were gathered, the family immediately set to work picking the ones a little higher up which were now ready. They worked the field over repeatedly like this until there was simply no more cotton left.

They had worked every day for more than a month, ex-

14

cept Sundays, of course. With a sigh of relief Mama stacked away all the pails and cans. Papa tied up the last bag, swung it over his shoulder and proceeded to take it away to the shed. Here the sacks were dumped into special burlap lined crates. These crates were filled with cotton, which in turn was pressed and stamped down by the heaviest person around. The burlap forms, now each holding about 80 to 100 kilos of cotton, were sewn up on top. Papa took the forms by wagon to the Loma Plata factory. From there, the processed cotton was ready to be shipped out to Asuncion, Paraguay, to Europe or anywhere else in the world.

It was now the end of April, and the job was done. The "year" had ended. Soon the May rains would come. Long, drizzly rains; rains that would spoil the cotton crop in short order if it hadn't been picked; rains that would bring with them a complete turn in the weather and, for Anna a change of lifestyle as well.

As she reflected, Anna told herself the year had been good. But looking ahead, she thought, "Maybe what is ahead will be even better."

May meant school. What excitement! School — the challenge of learning, the meeting of new friends, and the excitement of fun-filled activities.

Chapter Three

"ANNA," Mama called with a tone of impatience, "Anna, it's time to go! We can't be late."

The Rev. John J. Neufeld was preaching today, and excitement was in the very air. Adults and teenagers alike had been caught up in the spirit of revival. A new awareness of God and a sweeping desire for more fellowship, as well as commitment, had spread throughout the community. Anna, now fourteen and already graduated from school, was wholeheartedly in the midst of it.

Rev. Neufeld, a Canadian evangelist, had visited the area for the express purpose of encouraging revival among the believers. Most of them, in Schoenau and the neighboring areas, were believers, but were in a state of dryness, spiritual lethargy and a holding back that had been prevalent for too many years. The church, although the most important organ of the community, had majored on its own traditional forms. No Sunday school, Bible study, "Singstund"(1), or young people's activities had ever been offered. Many of the church-goers, especially the young, had only a very vague idea of what the 'faith' was all about.

The desire for more understanding and greater God awareness brought about some changes. Previously, the church services were only for Sundays. Now however, the occasional series of special meetings were held as men who seemed wonderfully knowledgeable in the Scriptures and filled with God's Spirit, were there to help them. Anna listened intently with the hunger of the undernourished, and loved it. Whatever she could understand, that is. Rev. Neufeld and

---

(1) An hour of planned but informal singing of hymns

16

Rev. John D. Friesen, both from Canada, as well as the internationally known Janz Team, were among these treasured guests.

The spirit of renewal was contagious and soon filled many with joy, enthusiasm and a new outlook on life. But it also brought pain. Not everyone was ready to accept this new spiritual enthusiasm and in some instances a fighting spirit broke out. This grew to the point where families had to make a major decision. Would they stick to tradition? Or would they accept renewal?

The climax of this dissension resulted in a deep internal split, although visibly the church remained intact. Anna, after hearing the various comments and versions of the problem, began to pray earnestly. She rejoiced when her prayer was answered just the way she'd hoped. Mama and Papa committed themselves to the side of renewal. That, Anna knew, meant at least two privileges. Their church would now offer a mid-week Bible study/prayer meeting as well as a "Singstund" on Saturday night for the young people. This was something to look forward to! Anna's action-loving heart sang with joyous excitement.

Even with the spiritual revival, the farm work could not be neglected. One day Mama, Anna and her brother Peter were on their little field, planting the winter garden of sweet potatoes. Papa was away, surveying for the much needed new road which would take them to Loma Plata. Anna, never wanting to appear weak, had debated for awhile whether or not to confess her stomach ache. The ache seemed so deep and persistent. Was it getting worse? She began to feel nauseated. Should she ask for permission to rest awhile?

Suddenly, there was no more hesitation! "Mama, my stomach hurts terribly," she fairly screamed through parched lips. She doubled over, moaning, as another spasm hit.

The potatoes were forgotten, as the three hurried inside. "You must get into bed at once." Mama's order was hardly spoken as Anna began to heave and retch. The orders became

17

more crisp and urgent. "Get Rev. Friesen, boys, and one of you get Uncle Wilhelm." The summonses were heeded with unusual haste. Rev. Friesen came immediately. He prayed with the family, a personal meaningful prayer from the heart of a man who knew God; a prayer that lingered long after he'd gone.

Uncle Wilhelm came with the horse and buggy. It didn't take him long to make a decision and put it into action. Anna was bundled up, and away they went, to the nearest little clinic, 15 kilometers away, at Hochstadt. Many silent prayers went up to God.

The man in charge at the clinic sprang into action! After a brief checkup he diagnosed acute appendicitis. Horseback riders were dispatched to locate Anna's Papa. Shortwave radio was used to contact the nearest doctor, who promised to come at once. The clinic personnel believed that Anna's appendix either had ruptured or was about to rupture.

"Give her medication for infection. Pack her in ice. And hang on till I get there," was the doctor's final word. But 130 kilometers is a long way, and recent rains had made the road nigh impassable. The homemade bus-truck that took him got stuck countless times, but they urgently pushed on through long hours of the day and all through the night.

More than 24 hours later the doctor arrived at Anna's bedside. Mama had sat there, watching, waiting, praying. Now, with a sigh of relief her lonely vigil was over. At last the doctor would take over.

Immediate surgery was demanded by the situation. A brief, local anesthetic was administered and then surgery was begun. It was a painfully long hour. The doctor got the tremendously inflamed appendix out in time, but in Anna's mind, the world had gone off track. Every thought was grabbed by pain, and soon became a formless muddle. Even Papa's welcome appearance on the scene helped only a little.

During the following days, however, Anna started getting better. Rev. Friesen came to sit with her one day. Among other things he asked her a big question that she wouldn't forget for a long time to come. "If you had not made it through this awful illness, would you have been ready to meet God?"

Anna was stumped and deeply troubled. That question she could not answer. Could anyone really know if he were ready to meet God? If so, on what basis? Was believing and praying the answer? Or was it a matter of being good enough? Did she measure up to the requirements? Was it even realistic to look for assurance? If so, why had she never been told?

She couldn't summon the courage to ask, so she pushed her questions aside. "Will I ever find the answer to my many questions?" she wondered vaguely as she drifted away into a fitful sleep.

"CAN I go to the mission today, Mama?" Anna asked. Thoughts of the mission had been on her mind a lot lately, and she felt a longing to be involved. When Mama consented Anna was overjoyed. The last time she'd been there something had pulled at her heartstrings, as if beckoning her to come back.

This time she witnessed a baptismal service at which some thirty native Lenguas were baptized. It struck her as being beautiful, yet very different. Quietly Anna sat there intently watching the round, brown faces, now slightly upturned, a bit childlike perhaps, but so utterly sincere as they made their commitments. A lump kept coming to her throat, and she quite forgot to give a second thought to the somewhat ragged, somewhat grimy clothes the Lenguas wore. And as for their bare feet, she never even noticed; they resembled too closely her own.

Because she did not know the language, Anna had ample time to let her mind wander. She recalled the numerous stories she had heard, the explanations of how this mission — such a strange venture — had begun.

Originally, when her people had settled in this country as pilgrims and strangers, but by full consent of the government, the land had been inhabited by the then uncivilized Lenguas. These Indians, living totally 'wild' lives, had been unprepared to fight for their rights legitimately, and found themselves pushed further and further back into poor land that nobody wanted. In this condition their plight worsened progressively. Who would take pity? Were they not people too, with living souls?

Before renewal had come to Schoenau and its neighboring communities, very few people had cared about the Lenguas. The handful who did, were sadly outnumbered, and struggled against tremendous odds to get some sort of 'mission' going. John M. Funk, a dear friend of Anna's parents, was one such pioneer. He had been the first resident to preach God's Word in the Lengua language. He did not believe in giving many handouts, but specialized in Bible teaching and practical assistance, helping the Lenguas earn their own livelihood. Many accepted his love and his teaching of a higher love. Lifestyle standards among them had risen tremendously, and now, with the revival of the church, support for this project increased dramatically.

This was the mission where Anna witnessed the baptismal service. Later she spent numerous occasions at the same mission. Always upon returning she found herself deeply thoughtful. "What believer, when he really walks with the Lord and wants to serve Him, can resist the challenge of spreading His love around to the less fortunate?" she would ask herself. "Surely it is only normal, only natural to do that much."

She was puzzled about the strange pull the mission had on her. Could it be that there was a force stronger than herself trying to get her attention, trying to point her along certain paths? And yet the question of whether she should become a missionary never entered her mind. That such a possibility even existed was beyond her comprehension. Nor was she aware that an individual must first make sure of his own salvation before sharing the Gospel with others.

At home, in the normal run of things, Anna found it easy to push such weighty thoughts away. She was a lover of fun and adventure, and every weekend she was sure to be in the midst of all the action.

Every Saturday night her gang, a group of some fifteen young people, would gather at church for 'Singstund,' a time for lusty and wholehearted singing. Making harmony was a new dimension, allowed since the renewal and it really added beauty and challenge to their hour. Before each person left for home, the group would gather outside for a friendly chitchat. Teasing and laughter permeated the air as they lingered to relish the joys of the moment. This was, after all, the highlight of their week; it was also the only source of amusement, sport or pleasure that the community offered its young people. Each, like Anna, was determined to savor it to the fullest.

On Sunday nights, they would gather in homes. Most of the time the houses seemed too small, hot and sticky. The young people would take all the available chairs outside and form a circle somewhere under the trees. These Sunday nights became very meaningful in many ways. The meetings turned into whatever the mood of the day demanded. Sometimes the young people discussed serious and weighty matters. Sometimes they sang for hours. Most often, however, their natural, fun-loving spirit took over. At such times games were the thing. Never realizing how limited their resources were, they joyfully played every game they knew: Drop the Hanky; London Bridge; Cat and Dog; Boy Chase Girl.

These Sunday nights afforded the young people their only chance for casual dating. The idea of coupling up was high on their priority list, just as it is in the minds of young people everywhere. In Anna's house this became a bit of a problem. She was the oldest, and Papa had high standards and strong convictions. Anna longed for 'freedom', and for a lively dating life. When she pleaded with him for permission to go out evenings during the week with one obvious intent, his answer was a very firm, "No." To her, it sounded harsh, almost cruel.

"When the right time comes, and a fellow knows what he wants, he will come here and ask," he stated in his most authoritative voice. There was no choice. She had to settle for it, but the struggle was intense. In the quiet of her own room, with clenched fists, she wept, throbbing with frustration and rebellion. Hours later, or the next day, she'd face the world again, and no one could guess the simmering feelings she hid so carefully inside.

One thing she had come to understand. The special reason she had for wanting to go out would have to be tucked away for now. Any dating she wanted to do would have to get squeezed in with the weekend socializing of the gang.

John had been eyeing her with admiration for some time and was beginning to show interest in all kinds of ways. He liked to sit next to her in the circle. He seemed to enjoy handing her things, getting her chair, helping her, walking together with her. Anna enjoyed the attention, the feeling of security, the thrill of hope for the future. Helen, her cousin, with whom she was very close, was also forming a relationship with a fellow called Peter. This added to the excitement. The two fellows were also cousins and good friends. There was in the air the promise of many wonderful times ahead.

Anna expected something, but didn't quite know what. John looked at her with such longing and deep feeling. Just thinking about him sent both shivers and thrills racing up her spine. A strange feeling of desire, a deep need for fulfillment, lingered often within her inner being. On the surface, however, Anna tried to protect the gaity and love-of-life spirit so typical of her.

One day things were different from the normal routine. For one thing, Papa wasn't home, so Mama was making the day special by spending it at her sister's house, which was Helen's family. Anna's only assigned duty was to help Mama take the younger children over there and bring them back again at night. This left lots of free time for Helen and her to spend together. How thrilled they were! But how to best use the time?

Helen and Anna walked the grounds. They sat on the corral. They talked. They laughed. They started feeling giddy and acting silly, as if something was letting them in on a secret without words; something special that they could feel but could not find words to describe.

That evening on the top rail of the corral, Anna whispered, "Let's call the guys." Immediately, like the night call of a homing bird, their own special whistles sounded through the darkness.

Within fifteen minutes both fellows appeared, pleased at the personal invitation. It was not the first time they had heard this call. But never had it held more than a playful meaning. Tonight however, it was a call for something more, something very special. The two couples sat together on the rails of the corral. The soft neighing of the horses just beyond added its own little bit of music to the tender moments.

"We'll have to go back to Helen's," Anna suddenly remembered. "Mama will be waiting for me to carry the little ones home."

"Then I'll walk you," John answered without any hesitation.

"Me too. We can all go," added Pete.

They slipped off the fence rails and headed for the path. Before anyone realized, a new pattern emerged. Two couples walked down the path, each hand in hand, each a bit apart from the other. The air was quiet and still. The deliberately slow footsteps blended with the soft murmur of voices, and the tender glow of the moon seemed to blow kisses in the air. The moments were tender, holy, too precious to waste.

All too soon Helen's house was right before them. The walk was over and the fellows had to leave. Helen turned to Anna.

"Guess what, Anna. Peter asked me to marry him. We are going to get married!"

"Us too! Us too!" Anna responded breathlessly.

"You too? Oh, I can't believe it! Is it really true?"

Helen couldn't believe it! But when they looked into each other's eyes, there were no more doubts. That sparkle could be trusted. They fell into each other's arms, hugging and embracing. It was the most sisterly thing that had every happened between them.

A nagging sensation stayed with Anna. On the one hand, she was sure — sure he was the right one meant just for her. On the other hand she was utterly filled with fears. What would the future hold? Would she be worthy? Would she be able to cope with whatever life would bring? The scary part made her feel so small, as though she needed Someone big and strong to really count on. She felt as though there were a vacuum inside that could not be filled, not even by the love of the one man she wanted above all others.

The social evenings of the gang were now replaced by exciting times for them alone. Let the others have their fun! To John and Anna these Sunday nights never came often enough; they were filled with joy, meaning, and fun. Time had a way of slipping by unnoticed.

Five months later, John came up with a bombshell. His parents, for personal reasons, had very unexpectedly decided to move to Bolivia. Because he was not yet twenty-one, John had to obey. His parents were the sole decision makers. There was no alternative, he must move along with his family.

Anna was stunned! This couldn't be true! She rebelled. She lashed out against the world. This terrible thing could not be happening to her! Just when things had been going so well, and she was sure she'd found real happiness, everything was all shattered. The only consolation was that John too was hurting and struggling. He too was stunned!

"Some day," he promised yearningly, "I will come back and get you. And, I'll write. I'll write as often as possible."

The day to say goodbye came far too quickly. And then, just as quickly it was gone. So was John. In three weeks they would be separated by 1200 kilometers.

As Anna plodded back to the house the most awful feelings of loneliness and despair engulfed her. It was as if darkness had overtaken her; there was no light on any horizon. Finally she got to her room. As she threw herself on her bed she burst into tears, crying as if all the frustration of all her years had let loose and turned into a heaving, tearing, spitting violence, which no power on earth could stop or control.

Gradually though, the sobs did grow quieter. Finally Anna was ready to reason a little. Not to accept, but rather to give God her little fist and demand an answer, "Why? Why? *Why?*"

Her resentment and bitterness stormed against the authority of parents. "Don't they understand? Don't they know that we are people too? That we have feelings?"

Eventually in frustrated despair, Anna lay quietly still. Finally she seemed ready to listen to whoever would speak sensibly to her. She sensed, more than heard, a still voice beside her. "I want *you*, Anna. Give yourself to Me in this struggle; trust Me with the answers and reasons."

"Give myself to God?" The question hurt, but it persisted. "Give myself to God? Haven't I? Haven't I always . . .?"

The question began to grab like a vise around her heart. Blindly she fought against it. Then slowly her vision cleared. "I've believed for a long time. I've thought about God. I've enjoyed singing about Him, and I've been interested in missions, . . . but have I ever given myself to Him?"

Suddenly she was on her knees. "Oh, God I *cannot* go on any longer. I cannot cope with life; it's too much. I can't go on."

For a moment everything was still, totally still like an interval between the booming crashes of a thunder storm. Anna felt she could not breathe. Should she risk the chance she was taking?

Suddenly she knew and immediately took a deep breath. Sink or swim, this was what she needed, what she wanted.

She had never understood it before, but now it became crystal clear. Hesitantly but very earnestly, she began to pray, "Please, God, could you take and accept me just as I am with all my sin and rebellion? I know I'm not worthy, but I do want to belong to You. If only You'll accept me. I want to belong to You and serve You for always and ever."

She couldn't quite explain the feeling that came over her. She sensed a giant weight being taken from her shoulders, she felt so light. At the same time she sensed a Presence, a comforting Something right beside her in the room. So personal and very real. Perhaps . . . why hadn't she thought of it before? This must be what that minister had called "born again." It simply must be! Hadn't he talked about "old things are passed away, all things are new"? That was her experience. But what could she call it. Few people talked about such things in her circles. One thing she knew — she'd never be quite the same again! A strange peace — it must be the heavenly kind — flooded slowly through her, and a new surge of inner strength filled her. Disregarding her tear-swollen face, she turned and picked up her faithful guitar. Her fingers fumbled for a moment, but only for a moment. Quickly an old song, the one she had always loved came through her fingers, with a depth and meaning she'd never known existed.

> Anywhere with Jesus I can safely go,
> Anywhere He leads me in this world below,
> Anywhere without Him dearest joys would fade,
> Anywhere with Jesus I am not afraid.
>
> Anywhere, anywhere! Fear I cannot know;
> Anywhere with Jesus I can safely go.
>
> Anywhere with Jesus I am not alone,
> Other friends may fail me, He is still my own.
> Tho' His hand may lead me over dreary ways,
> Anywhere with Jesus is a house of praise.

Mama heard, and the smile she gave Anna said more than her words ever would have. The smile declared, "I heard you weep and in my heart I wept with you. I see your tear stains but I'm looking deeper. I see a new joy bubbling out and I'm glad. I'm glad!" It was a benediction, like a rainbow after a storm. Tomorrow would be a new day — a whole new world to face! But for now it did not matter. Now only the newness mattered. With Jesus the rest would be taken care of.

The next Sunday the old gang came over, thinking she'd forget John and want to get involved in her former activities. The evening felt strange. In no way did Anna want to leave the impression that she was again free. Her commitment to John was real. The gang no longer had any appeal.

A few weeks after John had left, the Schoenau villagers were challenged by a new idea. It was so utterly new that people did not know just what to think. Cornelius W. Friesen had a vision for pioneering a brand new school in the community: a Bible school for young people. Soon a group of church "brethren" backed him, and they formed an organization to get this Bible school underway.

"Can I go?" Anna asked eagerly. "I'd just love to go!"

Papa looked at her keenly before he answered slowly, "I really don't know."

He couldn't hurry into such a big decision. For one thing, it would take money, and secondly, it would require the arranging of many details. The proposed site of the school was not within walking distance, not even within horseback riding distance.

Mr. Friesen came down to plead Anna's case. When Papa raised his objections, Mr. Friesen replied with great conviction, "If you would send your daughter to Bible school, it would be the greatest gift you could ever give her." That challenge grabbed Papa, and he changed his mind completely. Anna would go to Bible school, and he would support her, all the way!

To Anna the very idea of going to school presented a

whole new set of challenges. Since John had left, her socializing had dropped to a bare minimum. Instead of hanging around with the young people, she'd frequently go with Mama and Papa to visit their friends. She constantly felt like a fifth wheel. Finally there seemed to be a sun of hope appearing on the horizon, beckoning her.

Bible school opened the first of July. Anna was there, together with some twenty-five other young people. What joy and excitement! The fact that Helen was among the students added even more to Anna's already joyous enthusiasm.

The school itself was unique. The one-room building was packed with crude benches for the eager learners. If the young people could have compared their school with many a college across the world, their enthusiasm might have waned. As it was, they considered themselves most privileged. How could there be a problem, for were they not studying the basics of Scripture? Is that not why they were at school? Who would have wanted to be burdened with a load of detail, structure and perfection?

Anna loved school and never tired of drinking in new truths. Anything that stimulated her faith and encouraged her relationship with the Lord was just what she desired. There were, of course, times when a youthful spirit of gaiety, even frivolity, overtook her and the other students.

The school doubled as a dorm for those who lived farther out, which included three girls and the teacher. Each had brought a sleeping bag which was rolled out at night, after the benches were pushed together to form two "private" rooms. The usual amenities were missing — electricity, indoor plumbing, and other comforts of home. Uneven ground, oversized weeds and strewn logs decorated the yard. The students' cooking was done over an open fire under a shade tree beside the building.

One Wednesday night, Anna, Helen, and a few other local girls dashed out for a last moment of exercise and freedom. A spirit of laughter and merriment prevailed as they revelled in the delight of each other's company — until Anna tripped!

"Ow! ow! oh, shucks!" she groaned, sprawled out full length over a log.

Deciding to ignore the stabbing pain in her foot Anna gallantly got up. The total darkness made it impossible to see anything but she limped back to the other girls. She continued to scamper along with the girls, quietly pretending she wasn't hurt. Later, the teacher, noticing Anna's limp, looked at her foot. Was it ever swollen! He attempted to rub it, but that caused too much pain. Merely looking at it gave Anna goose bumps! "Look at all those bluish colors and the ugly swelling," she mused. "Was it broken? Sprained? Or what?"

"Oh, it's nothing," she blurted aloud. She wasn't about to admit defeat or engage in self-pity. "Let's just go to sleep and forget about it."

The fact that she couldn't sleep because of the pain was only for her to know. Morning finally came. Anna hopped around on one foot because the pain was too great if she put any pressure on the swollen foot.

On Friday after school, enroute home with the teacher and the three girls, Anna was taken to the local chiropractor. After examining the foot, he told her it was broken at the ankle and in the arch. He set it as best he could. Anna clenched her teeth and grabbed a chair so tightly her fingers were white. The pain was excruciating! Finally the chiropractor was finished. Anna felt greatly relieved. The foot got babied for some time, but as far as treatment went, that was the end of it. That God is the Author of healing was a truth Anna's people lived by literally.

JOHN and Anna had been corresponding regularly, once a week. Sometimes Anna kept a daily diary and sent it weekly. "Absence makes the heart grow fonder" proved true in their case. Their need for each other continued to grow stronger and stronger. John shared with her that he too had experienced a special encounter with the Lord. He wanted more than ever to give his life to the Lord.

His birthday rolled around. It was the all-important twenty-first. He had vowed that he would return to Anna, and in his letters he kept reminding Anna of his promise. Even before his birthday was quite there, he found himself enroute to Schoenau, telling himself, "At least I played my role as the eldest son. I've helped my parents get established in their new homesteading situation."

After John arrived in Loma Plata, he got a friend to take him to Schoenau on horse and buggy. Tired after the month-long trip, this last three-day section sapped his energy reserve. He came down with the flu. Instead of rushing over to Anna's as he'd planned, he went to bed at his sister's house. The news travelled fast, though. When Anna heard, she was in the middle of chores, caring for the cattle in the corral. She finished in record time, and hurried off to find John!

Flu or no flu, their joy was complete! They shared together freely, as they would continue in the days to come. One of the first things they decided was that both should get baptized. The fact that there were no others waiting to be baptized didn't matter. They were eager to take their stand publicly, and share their testimony.

JOHN was deeply in love but he was lonely. His homeless situation added to his loneliness. He *needed Anna.*

"Let's get married *now,*" he'd propose, with a strangely blended mixture of hesitancy and eager hope.

"But we had planned to wait, hadn't we? We are so young," Anna would protest. Then she'd think more deeply, and say, "What would we do? Where would we go?"

No matter which way the questions and answers got jostled, his final plea was always the same. "But I *need* you, Anna. Think about it. Couldn't we get married?"

Her heart had been so bruised and bleeding, she knew only too well what he meant. She couldn't say 'wait' much longer.

Broaching the subject to her parents was a more delicate thing. They were deeply concerned, and had a hard time letting their daughter go. They seemed to have deep inner misgivings about the move to Bolivia, which John was definitely planning. They were aware of the 'behind-the-scenes' reasons for the influx to Bolivia. However, they were unwilling to discuss these with the young couple. The fact that John had already bought land there did not set their minds at ease, but they did decide to let the decision be Anna's.

.Anna thought deeply before saying the final word. "I don't like the idea of moving away nor the prospect of living in Bolivia." John's decisiveness on that point bothered her a little, and yet. . . . "I can't bear the idea of separation either. If I say yes, we'll always be together. Really that right now is the important thing. . . . Wherever he goes, I will go."

She had made her decision, and when she told John, the joy on his face wiped out, for the time being at least, all traces of anxiety. And the squashing hug he gave her felt very right.

"You have made me very happy, Anna," he whispered tenderly. He seemed to be struggling with a lump in his throat, as he continued, "And . . . I . . . I must . . . always take care of you. . . ."

"For better or for worse," she mused that night, staring up at the ceiling with sleepless eyes. Her heart was beating fast and her whole body tingled with nervous excitement. "I have made the final decision, the final promise. It had *better* be for the better."

Then her thoughts went deeper, to the One who had been her precious One, her Help and Sustainer through every dark hour. This last year, walking close with God, had been so different, so worthwhile. She had learned so much. Somehow she knew afresh that His hand was holding her now, guiding her, protecting her, loving her. On the promise of His presence, she could let go and sleep in peace. All her tomorrows were in His hand.

Chapter Four

THURSDAY, July 12, 1958.

The big day had come at last. In some ways it came too soon. So very quickly it would be over, and then the beginning of the rest of her life would be upon her. Forever! Yes, forever! She'd be gone from Mama and Papa, facing an adult world, making a new life, a new home.

Anna had risen early, and stood now gazing at a perfect sunrise. Gorgeous, it seemed to her. Was this an indication of a wonderful future ahead? Questions had been tumbling around in her mind, disturbing her sleep and dulling for the moment the joy that should be so evident today. Had she really made the right decision? Would she not be sorry?

The promise of a beautiful day grabbed her, and began filling her with fresh joy and enthusiasm. For just one moment she closed her eyes to pray. "God, help us. Let it be right. Make it turn out. Please. You know I want to do Your will." And somehow she knew He would. A picture passed before her eyes, a picture of John and her stepping into a boat to go for a ride. The water seemed vast and the waves were high. The whole thing seemed very scary, until she realized Who was at the helm. *Why, God Himself was operating that boat!*

Had God sent those thoughts to her? Would you call it a vision, or was it only in her head? Was there anyone around whom she might dare ask?

"Anna, Anna," Mama was calling. It was time to get ready. The vague, wandering thoughts got shelved quickly and indefinitely, and in the excitement of the hour were soon forgotten entirely.

"I have to dress carefully today," Anna told herself, as she proceeded with the job. The new blue dress Mama had so lovingly helped her make looked just perfect as she studied herself in the chipped, little, wood-framed mirror. The new shoes she had bought, plain dark leather slippers, slightly pinched her toes. She didn't care. With time they would stretch, but today they only needed to look right. She focused her attention on her hair. She had new side combs with which to pin it back, but her hair seemed strangely stubborn. Several times she did and re-did it wishing for the curls that weren't there. Finally she combed it back and appraised it with an almost, satisfied smile. At last she was ready to meet her fiancé.

John's eyes glowed with compliments when he saw her. The natural blush accenting her cheeks and the mixture of shyness, joy and anticipation radiating from her eyes intrigued him. Only with difficulty could he restrain himself from hugging her tightly to himself, literally, out there in front of everyone. Now *that* would never have passed! The desire was pleasantly put aside until the quiet hours of the night would be upon them and all this 'schmuzzel' would be over. Wow!

For the present both John and Anna had to forget themselves personally, and concentrate on the day awaiting them. Many hours of hard work had already been given to make this day special. They must live it to the full!

All was in readiness. Many tarps, borrowed from neighbors, had been gathered, fastened to poles and formed into one huge tent on Anna's parents' yard. Underneath the canvas roof were the benches and tables, all set up. The large kettles of food prepared beforehand were already set out. Guests from far away arrived early and ate dinner with the family — komst borscht (1), plumi moos (2), bread, potatoes and yucca (3). The service, with more than 100 people in attendance, began at two. Rev. Friesen, their beloved minister, married them and preached a practical and personal message. The faspa (4), served at four, seemed a continuation of the noon meal with extra bonuses of coffee, butter, sugar and a variety of homemade sweets. All the guests had an enjoyable time. The evening's hearty sing-song by the young people served to crown the day and accentuate the young couple's deep inner joy.

John and Anna had become Mr. and Mrs. Wiens. It sounded right, and exciting too. God was good and so was the world that was now before them.

IT was time to get ready for the move to Bolivia. John refused to believe that the promise he'd made to his parents was unwise, and determined to keep it. Anna, just as determined to go with him regardless, valiantly pushed away the apprehension that nibbled at her mind. Even Mama and Papa helped in the preparations as they made gallant efforts to hide their concern.

The visas arrived! John and Anna's things were ready, and the last goodbyes had been said. Standing now in the back of the rusty truck box, with numerous others on similar missions, Anna dabbed away unwanted tears as the rattles of the big, old truck told her they were on their way. On their way to what? She reached out to wave one last time before they entered the curve ahead. New tears kept blinding her eyes. Could it be, she wondered vaguely, that an eighteen-year-old girl was after all too young to go away from everything and everybody she'd ever loved? Had her parents been right?

Suddenly she sensed John's breath close to her, his tall form giving her a feeling of strength, something to lean on. "I

---

(1) komst borscht — a thick hearty cabbage soup, Mennonite style
(2) plumi moos — a thickened sweet soup with prunes, raisins and other fruit, Mennonite style
(3) yucca — food made from the fruit of the yucca shrub adopted from local Indian cultures
(4) faspa — a Mennonite term for a light afternoon meal

am here," he whispered hoarsely, squeezing her hand. "And we are together. That's what's important," he added softly, yet with conviction. She took his proffered clean handkerchief and looked hesitantly up into his face. The love and adoration she saw there tugged at her heart, telling her the story that just now had needed repeating. For the moment it made her cry harder. Then it helped her stop. It was reassuring to think that his love was real. Yes, they'd make it! Together they'd make it.

Minutes later, more composed, but still snuggling closely to his strong shoulder, she sighed. Ignoring the several onlookers, she was ready to admit it. "Yes, we are together, and I'm glad. I know I can do it." In her heart she added, "And both of us belong to God. With Him on our side we shall surely make it."

Hand in hand they turned to join their fellow travellers. A sensation of expectancy and almost joy filled Anna. Why, perhaps this trip would even turn out to be fun!

THE truck pulled up at the roadside. Having travelled for three days, they had reached the border land area between Paraguay and Bolivia. It was time to camp again. Camp was a simple meal over an open fire and sleeping in a bedroll under the stars.

Before they were ready to sleep, they heard unusual noises. John got up and listened more intently. Biting his lips, he confirmed their fears. "That's it," he said. "That's the call of the Indians."

Clearly now all heard the call echoing through the jungle. One party was calling, the other answering. Were they telling each other that they'd heard or sensed the presence of the white man? Goose bumps and shivers crawled up Anna's spine. This was the country of the Ayoré, a tribe that was totally uncivilized, wild, barbaric. She had heard about them. What would the Indians do? What would happen? Anna gave an involuntary shiver as these anxious thoughts flooded her mind.

It didn't take a long discussion for the weary travellers to decide what to do. And, it didn't take long either to get back onto the road for more travel. The night's rest was forgotten as they drove hastily out of the area.

John's face had a faraway look as they bumped, jiggled and rattled along. He was thinking deeply, Anna could tell, and she waited for him to explain. Both were wide awake, and the time seemed right for sharing.

"You know," he began quietly, "this incident reminds me very much of an experience I had here when I came back to get you, Anna."

He was warming up to the story. "I was riding in a truck with two Bolivians, and right about here the truck broke down. We decided that if we could find enough wire, we could fix it. We knew there was lots of stranded wire along the border — remnants of the war, you know. We started looking and found a little, but we needed more, and decided to search deeper into the jungle.

"As we pushed along through the vines and thick undergrowth, we realized suddenly that we were entering a clearing."

The other travellers had caught snatches of the conversation and strained to listened. Every eye was intently upon him now. John took a deep breath. "Suddenly we were face to face with three hunting Manjui Indians. Nude, but fully armed, they advanced sternly and stoutly toward us. My Bolivian friends backed up and hid behind me. My first thought was, 'God, save me. Help me. What do I do?' And then, very clearly, I felt Him give me calmness and clarity of mind. I remembered suddenly the little things I'd always been told to do. I smiled. *I smiled a long smile at them,* and I could sense that they were relaxing just a little. I lifted a piece of our wire and with unofficial sign language explained to them what I wanted. For long minutes they eyed me warily. Then they huddled together for a consultation of their own, and soon gestured for us to follow them deeper into the jungle.

"I tried to suppress my apprehension. I realized that, unarmed, we were totally at their mercy whether we followed or not. We might as well trust them and follow.

"They took us to a place where there was much more wire, and urged us to take as much as we wanted. Then they escorted us back to the truck. Had they watched us earlier and known right along we were there? The thought gave us the shivers. . . . Well, we gave them some gla'te (5). Their smile was genuine as they recognized our appreciation. Quietly and quickly they disappeared back into the jungle."

John sighed as if he were finished. Everyone sat in hushed silence. Then John began again, in a voice that was low and deep, and holding a hint of anguish. "What I can't understand is why nobody, *absolutely nobody,* is in there to help the poor people? They ought to have a chance too. . . ." His voice trailed off into nothing.

Anna shifted her position, trying to find a more comfortable spot. She looked at John. Something about his words stirred up the old feeling inside — the strange inexplicable tug at her heart. Anna moved again, hoping the change would clear her mind and remove that strange feeling; the feeling she'd first noticed at the Lengua Mission back home. Why should it follow her here? She couldn't understand it and certainly didn't like it. It was too vague and scary.

IN Bolivia they changed their travelling style and continued by train. They put their belongings among the crates and boxes of one of the front cars, and found themselves spots to settle into. This steam-engined freight train, old and heavily laden, climbed and wound along. The pulling got harder and the sparks flew higher. Suddenly to John and Anna's bewilderment and fright they saw flames leaping from the

_____

(5) gla'te — small hard homemade buns, Spanish style

roof of their car. What could they do! Frantically they tried to put out the fire. The hustle and bustle became a nightmare! The passengers rushed around in hectic efforts to save belongings. Finally some men climbed on top of the car and put out the fire with water. Some of the stuff inside had begun to burn. What wasn't burning was soon soaked with water. During all this the train never even stopped!

When they had started out, a soldier on train duty had asked if anyone had gas or such like in the car. Everyone insisted, "No!" Now when the danger was over, one man pointed to his ten-liter container of gas. John and Anna shuddered. "What if. . . ."

"But," mused Anna, "God answered our prayers. In fact, this just proves how very much God loves us and is with us right here."

Her faith was encouraged. However, when she noticed that the beautiful quilt her mother had so painstakingly made for her as a farewell gift was half burned and completely ruined, she almost lost that vision. In a wave of disappointment she struggled intensely for several minutes, choking back some half-sobs, and asking, Why? Very shortly though, she again became more encouraged. "God knows about it. He loves me and is here with me now."

IN Santa Cruz John's parents welcomed them and had them move in with them. Soon John and Anna were pellmell into the activities of trying to establish a farm of their own. The work was strenuous, with seeming obstacles constantly in the way. As the material problems multiplied, the struggle in Anna's heart multiplied even more.

Neither John nor Anna had realized the reason behind the influx of their people to Bolivia. His parents' reason had been personal, but everywhere else John and Anna went, they were bombarded with comments, criticisms and negative withdrawing attitudes that totally unnerved them. To think that Christians (she fervently hoped they were!) had actually moved here to escape the renewal of the church — *to avoid "modernism" like Singstund, Bible study, and missions!* Suddenly it hit Anna! Others might think that they too had moved to Bolivia for that reason. She couldn't bear it! Why, it was the direct opposite of their own dreams and convictions, and she was convinced they would never settle in happily. *They had come to the wrong place!* Sadness hung over her like a cloud. Pallor and emptiness replaced the once cheerful outlook and life became one long drag.

She talked about it to John. He felt the same way, but was torn between the desire to please his parents and be at peace in the neighborhood, or to follow his personal convictions and have a happy wife as well. He just didn't know what to do. Outwardly he carried on as though nothing had changed.

One day Anna could bear it no longer. The few months she'd been in Bolivia seemed forever; the emotions she'd tried so *maturely* to suppress were festering inside, waiting for the slightest trigger to erupt; and visions of Mama and Papa came ever before her causing the waves of homesickness to engulf her.

"John," she announced as they sat at dinner, eating from crudely made dishes in the half-finished house, "I have made my decision."

He saw her deep agitation and waited for her to continue. "I . . . I have decided I cannot live here. If you must, you must, but I cannot. I will go back home. I will find a way to go, and leave as soon as I can. I'm sorry about hurting you, but I see no other way."

For a moment he just sat there immobilized by shock. The set look on her face told him that she meant every word. Why had he not realized how serious the problem really was? Finally his mind could again function. Rather shakily, but resolutely, he got up, walked toward Anna and gently pulled her to himself. He did not have the answers. But one thing he knew, *he loved her, and he was by no means prepared to let her go.*

39

Holding her tightly, he whispered fervently, "Let's pray. Let us pray like we've never prayed before. God will give us an answer. God must give us an answer! *But you will not go back alone!* Whatever we must do, we will do together."

After a seeming eternity, John released his grip on Anna, slowly turned and walked away. To Anna his decisive words, a greater encouragement than he could ever imagine, spelled relief. To fight, to kick against the pricks, was such a tiring thing. Perhaps now she could rest. She longed, like nothing else, to lay her head on someone's shoulder and cry herself to sleep. She longed to rest without a worry. . . .

John had said to pray. Finally she was willing to give the whole problem to God. She slipped onto her knees and, between the sobs, poured out her story to the One who always listens. Slowly it dawned on her that God knew. He knew! And cared! Yes God could and would solve the problem. He would show John, or do *something!* A new peace flooded over her, and she thought, "Why, somewhere the sun is shining. Maybe soon it will break through my clouds too."

JOHN could not concentrate on the job he'd been doing. He would have to make some kind of decision. His whole being demanded that he sort out his thoughts. His first option — to remain here and make a go of things — seemed firmly closed. He doubted very much that there was any chance of things changing. Without that, their days were numbered. He pulled out his second option and tried to face it. It wasn't pleasant. Give up? Quit? Go home and thereby tell everyone, that they couldn't hack it? That he couldn't control his wife? That between them, they were too weak, too. . . .?

"Oh, God," he cried in anguish, lifting his face heavenward. "Is there no other way? Don't you have a plan somewhere for us, something . . . anything . . .? *Help me to find Your will and do it. I want to do Your will, God.*"

Suddenly peace began to fill him. The thought, "God will show us the way," grabbed hold of him and remained. The heaviness of the burden was strangely gone.

"I don't know how, but I've received the assurance that God is preparing a third option for us. Let's just wait a bit and see," he assured Anna that night.

She relaxed. It was good to give in to God and wait for Him. It was good to give in to her husband and trust him to make the right decision. It was good. . . . Nestled closely against him, she fell asleep more peacefully than she had for many a week.

Five days passed. A feeling of expectancy permeated her being. Despondency could not rule her now, but questions lurked around every corner. Would God really answer? How? And when? Waiting had always been such a hard thing.

SENSING a bit of commotion outside, Anna looked out through the window. Something different was happening. A jeep holding total strangers, a man and a woman, had driven up and stopped in front of John's parents' house. They appeared to have come for something and were being invited inside. Unsettling shivers of excitement crept up and down her back. What could they possibly want? And why should their coming cause such excitement in her?

The story that soon emerged was, to John and Anna, totally spellbinding. The couple represented a mission at Tambo, a place near Cochabamba in the Andes Mountains. "New Tribes Mission," they said it was. Apparently the work at Tambo, a missionary children's school, was only one of many stations the mission had in the country. It was understaffed and they had been having special prayer for more personnel.

At this point, for some inexplicable reason, the workers had received an overwhelming conviction that they should come to this very area in search of a young Christian couple to help them out at the station. They seemed to have no doubt but that the young couple was here. *Their only job was to find them!* It sounded like the story of Jacob's servant in search of a wife for Isaac!

John and Anna looked hard at each other. Could this be it? Was this the answer they were awaiting from God? It seemed too incredible.

Anna, always prone to be impulsive, decided, "Yes, it must be. This must be God's answer!" Her heart almost skipped some beats as she pondered it. Wasn't it exciting to see God lead?

John wanted a little more time to think and pray. One had to be very sure, he reasoned, before jumping into such a brand new venture. Anna's argument that 'anything would be better than this' was not enough. But the thrill of seeing such a spectacular answer from God overwhelmed him too and it wasn't long before he made a decision. He was convinced it was directed by God. *They would go to Tambo.*

The abruptly changed plans called for property to be sold and belongings to be reorganized. This added up to three weeks packed with fluttering activity and eager anticipation. John's parents had realized earlier that Anna would not be happy in their village. They accepted the fact that the young couple could, after all, not be expected to settle down here, and raised no further objection.

SETTLING in at the mission school was an adventure in itself. They were assigned a neat little house of their own — a first in their short, rather turbulent marriage. The work, although often demanding, was stimulating and exciting.

The school, with seventy, white, mostly American children, was indigenous or trying to be. John's main task was farm work. He put in long hours on the field, planting and harvesting or working at the many other duties necessary to accomplish the giant project of supplying the compound with all its food.

Anna's duties varied: help in the kitchen and dining hall was always needed, then there was laundry to do. The teacher couples soon discovered that she was an excellent babysitter as well, and began to make use of that talent.

Being busy was something Anna was used to from her childhood. Being needed was something she always longed for and thrived on. And being at a place, on a *mission for God,* was something that agreed with the deep secret desires of her heart. For both her and her husband the months rolled by rather quickly. It was indeed, a very happy time.

To add to the excitement and happiness that filled their lives, Anna came home from the doctor one day with special news. She was pregnant! Oh, joy, what an added blessing. Indeed it seemed to complete and crown their first year of joyful service. Looking forward to such a special new adventure put extra zest and sparkle into their lives.

The first eight months of her pregnancy went by uneventfully, and Anna continued her work. At Los Negros, station with a leprosarium and a hospital, the New Tribes Mission had a lady doctor. As she kept tab on Anna's health, the doctor became really interested in her case and insisted that Anna have the baby at the hospital. Los Negros, however, was eighty kilometers from Tambo, and that meant one and a half hours travel. This, claimed the doctor, left them with only one alternative. Anna must come and stay with her where she'd be close to the hospital whenever the need arose.

Anna didn't like that idea at all. "Do I *have* to go, John?" she asked repeatedly.

He looked at her. "You don't want to go, do you?"

"No, I hate the very thought. I'm away from the family already, and now to go away from you as well. It just isn't right. At a time like this we should be together. Surely, it's our thing together — not just mine." Without wanting to, she had raised her voice and the words came out sounding sharp-edged, slapping John. Perhaps her instinctive but hidden fear of the delivery experience was part of the reason.

With the hurt clearly written on his face, John turned to her, "It wasn't my idea, and I'm not going to make you go. But it seems to me they want what's best for us, for you, for the baby. And that's what's important. Your health and safety are important to me.''

Anna was sorry — sorry she'd hurt him. Still, she wondered, was it necessary that she go? Was it right?

Several staff members began using their best persuasive powers. They certainly seemed to think it was both necessary and right. Finally, with John's encouragement she decided to go.

For Anna this was the beginning of a very turbulent time. Being away from John, who was kept busy at the Mission, as well as from everyone else, it seemed, brought new waves of loneliness. Like never before, she longed for her mother's presence. Whenever she thought of the big day so soon to be upon her, this longing became acute pain. Nagging doubts and questions began to torment her again, and it was only when she was able to commit everything to God that she gained some semblance of peace.

There was one aspect of this stay, however, that was most appealing to her. The doctor had invited her to become an assistant helper in the hospital. She found those hours most rewarding. In fact, ever since the time of her appendectomy, she had felt a secret urge to become a nurse. She'd never told anyone and kept the desire nicely hidden, but now it surfaced and gave her joy — joy that mingled into the loneliness she struggled with — and helped her keep an emotional balance.

With only a normal amount of ado, son Arthur arrived a bit late one Sunday morning, weighing in at nine pounds and twelve ounces. John was informed via radio and by evening he was there to make the new family circle complete, soothing, at least temporarily, the ache in Anna's heart.

On the fifth day after Arthur's birth they returned to Tambo together, ready, and yet not ready to take up the work again. Anna's doubts and homesickness refused to leave. Her weakened, post-natal condition was ripe ground for such emotions. This became even more acute as she battled a physical ailment — malaria.

At the age of nine Anna had experienced a seizure of

malaria. In all the healthy, active years since she'd almost forgotten. Now however, the chills, sweat and fever persisted, leaving her utterly weak and exhausted. Even after the medication had taken effect, a tired listlessness prevailed.

She would have refused to believe it had anyone told her that this was merely a relapse of her former malaria, and that it was setting a precedent for many more relapses in the years ahead — relapses always waiting, ready to spring an attack on her at the most vulnerable moment. No one warned her, and neither she nor John worried about it.

John did constantly see her pale pinched face, however, and knew that something must be done. Together they decided, quite suddenly, to pack up and go home to Paraguay to Anna's family. Perhaps such a tonic, to cure the homesickness, would also do much to perk her up physically. It was certainly worth a try.

Many varied thoughts kept them company enroute home. To sort them out was impossible. The fervent protests from the staff at Tambo still rang in their ears. No one there had seemed to agree with them or appreciate their impulsive decision. Very obviously the needs there were not over; there was much work to be done. They were convinced that the work had been for God. They felt right about that. But where the matter of finding God's will for their own lives came in, they did not understand. After their earnest pleas to God two years ago, He had miraculously shown them where to go. Now, however, couldn't common sense tell them it was time to move, to go home? Wasn't that enough?

Neither John nor Anna had ever been taught or counselled to *wait* upon the Lord for guidance or consciously to put their decision-making under His sovereign will. That subject was almost foreign to them and most hazy. The fact that they had stumbled into that direction last time around was, if not totally accidental, at least a product of the pressure of their extreme need and deep heart's cry. God had been gracious. Like a father of beloved young children, He had simply and kindly shown them their path.

But that was then, not now.

At one point during their stay at Tambo they had struggled with the desire to become full-time missionaries. Now, in reflection, the memory became very vivid. One of their friends had begun to make arrangements for them to go to Bible school. Then after discussing it with another couple who told them, "People of Mennonite background don't make good missionary material," they had become discouraged and given up the idea. . . . If God had wanted them to become missionaries, wouldn't He have revealed it to them in some special way? Didn't He *call* people for such work? Well, He hadn't! Why think about it? Wasn't it absolutely reasonable to presume that it was His will to forget about it, and now at last make their own way in this world? Wasn't it sufficient that they had given Him two active years of their lives? It could not be otherwise. It *had* to be right.

Chapter Five

"HERE we are, Anna," John announced with a flourish as they entered the familiar village. Even though Schoenau had not changed much over two years, John didn't take note of the sameness. No, he was intently watching Anna. What would these homey surroundings do for her? John waited to see her reaction. Gradually a big smile spread across her face belying her recent attitude, and hiding for the moment the wan look on her face.

A sigh of relief escaped John as he thought "That alone is worth coming home for."

The reunion was indeed beautiful, tender, and worthwhile. Tears of joy flowed frequently as the two families spent days getting reacquainted. The eager smiles hid the fact that Mama and Papa had aged during John and Anna's absence. This atmosphere, along with Mama's excellent cooking, soon helped Anna out of her lethargy. She perked up amazingly, and soon was her normal self again.

Little Arthur, thriving on the loving care, grew rapidly. He was a special crown of joy to the proud young grandparents, as of course, to John and Anna.

After a few happy weeks with her parents, Anna and John were ready to move on and seek to establish a place of their own. They decided on Loma Plata, a well-established little town, and before long were able to move into a house.

The year was 1960. John was able to get a job with the local Co-op. Because 'advanced' modern machinery had changed the scene rapidly from a few years back, John was able to become a tractor operator. His work included combining for the farmers, plowing, as well as the always exciting job of digging water holes — dugouts for the cattle on the farms. This he did with a large drag-line type of machine.

47

Financial success seemed a definite possibility as John looked at the future. Although his wages were quite moderate, the Lord's blessing seemed on them.

"Let's build a house of our own," he popped at Anna one evening.

"Really? Can we?"

"I think we can. At least quite shortly we should be able to. We have enough now to make a good start."

That sounded good. And, it sounded like fun. Many evenings they'd sit together and plan. Anna would get out some pencils and paper so they could sketch away, first dreaming and then slowly but surely changing that dream to reality.

In accordance with the popular style in the area, they settled for a bungalow. They designed it in two sections. Because of the heat from cooking, and the tremendous insect attraction in this area, the kitchen and dining room were one section out toward the backyard. Three bedrooms and a pleasant living room, facing the front, was the other section.

Anna loved the house. "It's exactly what I've wanted," she confided to a friend who dropped in. "I feel secure here, and happy."

To herself she added afterward, "Maybe I'm biased, but to me it is even beautiful." Perhaps the fact that this house became her haven of rest through many storms and struggles, explained partly why she held it so dear.

The family was growing in more ways than one. Arthur was scarcely weaned, when Albert came along. Two years later Rachel joined them, and then in 1965 the twins, Veronica and Monica, filled the air with excitement and endless hours of duty.

Each of the children was a blessing — a wanted child. The saying Anna had heard, 'Children come like weeds in the garden,' was certainly not true for them. Anna loved each one, and whenever she'd have a spare minute she'd breathe brief prayers to God for them. Prayers for their protection, development and guidance, and especially prayers that each would in due time make a real and personal commitment to God.

Physically, however, child-bearing brought some pretty stiff battles. After each baby, during her postnatal recuperation period when her natural vitality reached an especially low ebb, she would come down with malaria. It seemed each time was a little worse than the last. Thanks to the doctors, drugs, and hospital now available to them, each bout lasted only for a few weeks, and then she was well again, hopefully for good.

·When she was back to her normal self, she resumed her household duties with joy, frequently singing while going about her work. One old favorite hymn would come to her most often:

Take Thou my hand and lead me unto the end;
In life and death I need Thee, O blessed Friend;
I cannot live without Thee for one brief day;
Lord, be Thou ever near me, and lead the way.

Thou mighty God of ages, O be Thou near;
When angry tempest rages I need not fear;
Close to Thy side abiding I fear no foe,
While Thy strong hand is guiding life has no woe . . .

Yet every so often, and she noticed it more often lately, she'd sense a restless gnawing somewhere deep inside. She couldn't define it. Could it be that although the family fulfilled a great need in her life, she was destined for something beyond it? Did it have something to do with her secret desire for nursing and medicine, which she could never quite successfully erase from her mind? Or did it have to do with the pull she used to feel when she thought of missionary work and the tremendous needs of the many unreached tribes around them? Could there possibly be a connection between these various possibilities?

Never could she seem to bring such jumbled thoughts to any sort of conclusion. For one thing, she was too busy. The cycle of dishes, diapers or wiping dirty noses seemed never to end, and times allotted to the sorting out of thoughts were pitifully few. Then too, because of John's new job as bus driver, he was hardly ever home. This afforded little time to talk things through. Frequently the run, from Loma Plata to the capital, Asuncion, would keep him away for a whole week, and on some occasions even up to ten days. The highway was unpaved, and a rainy spell could put it into a most deplorable condition. Waterfilled ruts, pot holes and bits of quicksand were the order of the day on such runs. The delays were too numerous to count. Frequently, too, the government regulations forbade traffic to continue after heavy rains, forcing John to sit for days and simply wait.

In spite of the problems John liked the job. And, it paid well. Anna didn't really mind; she enjoyed seeing John happy even if it meant a bit of a sacrifice. She recalled her first feeble efforts at conquering loneliness, and realized she had learned a lot since then. Perhaps she was growing up. At any rate she found nothing to regret. Their marriage was good, their income was reliable, their house was nice and their family was all healthy and doing fine. What more should a woman ask?

Anna would preach little sermons to herself, "I should be ashamed to even wonder about it. Why, I have so much to be thankful for." And it seemed only right that she should quench the nagging little voice inside her. Besides, she reasoned one day, if God were trying to tell her something, would He resort to such vague ways?

One night she prayed, "God, please solve this feeling of restlessness way down in my heart. You know that I am really very happy and thankful." She paused, fumbling for the right words. "If . . . if there ever is something you want to tell us, please tell us clearly, so we know for sure."

Nothing happened.

Little did she realize what an answer to such a prayer

might mean. Nor had she ever stopped to think that by the very means of that small voice God might already have been trying to get her attention. Was He?

It was December 6, 1966. Little Freddie, their sixth baby, had arrived. Although Freddie was cute and precious, his arrival brought trouble. Anna had another relapse of malaria. This time it came sooner, hit harder and lasted longer. While she lay day after day on her hospital bed, the doctors and nurses struggled with a seemingly hopeless task. For some reason none of the usual medication took any effect. She was getting worse instead of better.

John had considered the possibility of her becoming ill, but, with optimism born of previous experience, he had chanced another bus run. On his return, however, the house was empty! (The children had been taken in by kind neighbors). Alarmed and unsure, he hurried to the hospital not knowing what to expect.

The doctor confronted him with the news, "Your wife is very, very ill."

When John questioned him, the doctor continued most gravely, "Nothing has helped. The medication that has always worked is not doing a thing. We . . ."

Anxiously John awaited his next words. Why was the doctor stalling? "We. . . . we don't expect her to make it through this day. If she does . . . *If* she does, I say, that might be an indication that she'll rally and pull through."

"No, Lord. Why . . . why now . . . why was I not home?"

Heavy at heart, with prayers that were deep but unspoken, John eased down beside her. Was she unconscious or merely asleep? Finally, he took her hand, squeezed it, and received a slight response. Encouraged, he whispered, "Anna, I'm here. Can you hear me?"

Her heavy eyelids fluttered open. Their gentle flicker told John that she knew and bade him welcome. With a deep sigh Anna turned and covered her eyes with her hand. If she weren't so tired, she could talk. If . . . if this terrible headache

51

would go away, maybe she could at least think.

That headache had been a cruel companion before. Each malaria relapse had brought with it a long and severe ache. Lately the headaches had recurred more frequently. And at most unexpected times. When really severe, they had affected her so totally that it had alarmed her. At such times she could not for the life of her remember things — not even the names of her children or a hundred other things she had always taken for granted.

Now this headache had persisted for . . . oh, she couldn't remember. Was it days or weeks or months? Time had lost all meaning. To her right now, time simply wasn't.

It would seem so natural, so easy, just to slip away and be gone. It seemed that Someone somewhere was beckoning her too, but then the sense of John's presence beside her seemed to call her back. The touch of his hand had a strange pulling effect, telling her to hang on. As if she had a reason somehow to hold on and fight. Did she? Must she resist the temptation to let go and fall asleep, to let go . . . and . . . fall asleep . . . to fall asleep . . .?

Something nudged her! Was it John's hand? Had someone spoken? She felt the urge to rouse, to pay attention. Suddenly floating before her eyes, she saw their children, one by one. They were calling her. *They needed her.* A groan escaped her swollen lips. If she mustered *all* her strength, *all* her old will power, could she make it? Could she live? "No!" her tired body screamed. "It can't be done. No resources left. You're completely finished."

She slumped lower on the pillows as she felt herself go limp. The room became deathly still — as still as her too-quiet body. John held his breath. Was it going to end like this?

Anna's body shivered as another deep, anguish-filled groan escaped her. A fleeting memory of an old Bible story passed in front of her eyes. Wasn't it Jacob who had wrestled with an angel? Hadn't that struggle been long and hard? Was that what was required of her — a wrestling spirit?

She found herself praying quietly but frantically. "Oh, God, I can't make it. I can't . . . But . . . my children . . . could you please . . . could you please . . . do a miracle . . . so I could . . . so I could teach my children . . . about You? Could you . . . could you let me live so long . . . till I have seen my children . . . turn to You . . . to follow . . .?"

The prayer dwindled off into nothingness but the next groan was not quite so full of anguish. Anna opened her eyes just long enough to see the longing and love written all over John. A new sense of peace flooded through her, like a ray of light in a dark room, before her consciousness faded once more into oblivion.

John had heard only the groans. "Oh, God," his prayer became more fervent. "Save her! *Save her!* For me. For the children. We need her!"

The nurses checked her pulse and blood pressure. Very soon they were back to check them again. Then again. She was holding her own. Again, yes still holding on. Again. Was there an improvement . . . ever so slight?

The doctor came in. This time he was hopeful. "She might be over the worst. If she keeps on this way, there is a chance. Yes, she has a fighting chance."

Day and night John kept his "watch and pray" vigil. Slowly Anna recovered. In spite of the frequent little setbacks that had everyone holding his breath, each day seemed a wee bit better.

One day the doctor had a serious, decisive talk with John. Grimly he declared, "One thing is certain, Mr. Wiens. You *cannot* go on like you are if you want to keep your wife. For one thing she must *never* have another baby . . . Secondly, you must get her out of this country, totally out of this climate. You'll have to move away somewhere, any place, that has no malaria. United States. Canada. Somewhere!"

The doctor paused, took a deep breath, then continued in a softer voice, "I hate to do this, but I have to tell you the truth. If you don't move out . . . her days here are numbered.

She may live for a year, maybe two." He shrugged. "I can promise you nothing, nothing hopeful for the future! Only time will tell. Anna may recover and seem to be quite well, but if in her condition she has another relapse . . . and we have nothing to give her. . ."

John hardly heard these final words. So this was how it was. The news was disconcerting and baffling. What should they do? What could they do? To move to a strange new country with a new culture, new language, new everything, was not a small thing. Not when you had a sick wife and six little children. And, no promise of a job.

As Anna improved John was tempted to forget the doctor's grave words. Could things *really* be that bad? And yet the longer John thought about it the clearer the decision became. Since he knew the facts, he could not stay here. It simply would not do. He had no desire to take that kind of risk.

LIKE a sharp U-turn or a hairpin curve on a road, another new chapter had begun in John and Anna's life. God had spoken. They knew it, and wanted to hear it, despite the fact that it was not easy to sell a well-loved house, quit a good job, and pull up all their stakes in the community in favor of an unknown future. But it had to be done.

Manitoba, Canada became their destination. The homeland of their grandparents would now become theirs. Then too, John's parents had recently moved there from Bolivia. Their letter sounded encouraging. In a village called Grunthal they had found a house and property that suited them and, together with the younger members of the family, were settling in comfortably.

John and Anna were kept too busy to worry much. The various preparations involving paper work, selling property and the arranging of the many details for the trip took a lot of time. Finally the big day arrived. Saying goodbye to Anna's parents was hard, but at last even that was done. Only the future remained. And that unknown future, alluring though it was, looked suddenly more than a little scary.

Anna's heart beat fast as they climbed the narrow metal stairs to the plane. Never before had she flown. Neither had John, nor the children. None had an inkling of what the trip would be like.

Would the children fuss embarrassingly, or become air sick perhaps? Would the border crossings be hopelessly difficult? Did Canada actually want them? Would their own fragile health last through the strenuous days ahead? Might their no-English language barrier become an insurmountable problem? A thousand questions appeared on Anna's horizon, mocking her.

Each time she'd become frustrated, however, she handed her doubts and frustrations to John. He seemed so capable. Was he really so confident, or did he merely hide his fear?

Every stop marked a lap that was finished; every fresh flight one step closer to their destination. Things were going well. Anna was feeling comparatively strong, and several of her questions had been settled favorably. After they entered the United States, however, a new misgiving began to taunt her.

"Something's wrong, John," she whispered, puzzled. "People are *staring* at us."

He hadn't noticed, but now he began to watch. Surely Anna must be imagining things. Before long he changed his mind. "Yeah, I guess they are," he admitted, shrugging his shoulders. "But I sure wouldn't know why." Nonchalantly he turned back to his magazine.

But Anna couldn't forget. It felt like a premonition, warning her of trouble ahead. She asked herself, Why? It couldn't be their clothes, could it? They were wearing their best. Was their family too large? Back home it hadn't been. What was so noticeably different about themselves, eight well-tanned Paraguayans, among all these North Americans? Perhaps . . . It would be several years until the answer to her puzzle would dawn on her, and she could enjoy it with a hearty chuckle.

For now she simply had to shelve the concern.

The plane landed once more. They had arrived at their destination — Winnipeg. Excitedly, but anxiously, they filed out — Anna holding baby, Freddie, with Rachel clinging to her creased cotton skirt, John with a twin in each arm and Arthur and Albert close behind. Would someone be there to meet them?

Thankfully, Anna spotted John's parents waiting at the terminal to welcome them. The joy of seeing each other dispelled for the moment the questions hanging so stubbornly on John's and Anna's minds. For now, just the assurance of family closeness was all that was needed. The parents' old two-storey house on Main Street in Grunthal had ample space to keep the family for the next while.

They had made it here. For better or for worse. John and Anna were in Canada, ready to become all-out Canadians.

"It had better be for the better!" John muttered to himself, staring out the window at the unfinished village street below. "It just better."

His puckered frown, however, quickly changed to a smile when Anna slipped up beside him. It wouldn't do to add his fears to hers. She had enough. Instead he grabbed her by the waist and spun her around as he hugged her to himself. As her feet lifted and swung in the air, she couldn't help but laugh. She went round and round, her laughter filling the room and soon mingling with John's. He set her down with a lighter heart. Nothing, absolutely nothing, could cheer him like Anna's pleasant laughter. Always it was worth the making.

Chapter Six

SETTLING into a new country was quite the adventure. English was a totally foreign language; they spoke Spanish, German and the Low German dialect still so typical among descendants of the traditional Dutch Mennonites. The fact that they found many friendly people, including relatives, who spoke the latter two, made things a lot easier.

After shopping around and looking at numerous properties, John came upon a house in the village of Niverville, some 35 kilometers south of Winnipeg.

"Come and see it," he urged Anna. "I think you'll like it."

Almost at once Anna fell in love with the place. Although the house was tiny, it was neat and fairly new. The basement was fixed up for extra bedrooms, and the modern conveniences, though compact, were all there. A feeling of awe overcame her. "Like a little bit of heaven," she whispered fervently.

They didn't wait long to make up their minds. The purchase went smoothly. To furnish the house they shopped at secondhand stores and also gladly accepted several gifts.

Someone had a lovely shower for Anna, which practically filled the empty kitchen shelves. When row after row, jar after jar and box after box had been neatly put away, she stepped back to appraise the result, and called, "Hey, John, kids, come and look. See what we've got!" Indeed, those filled shelves looked rich and alluring, especially to the boys who were soon planning how to get into the attractive jars, hopefully without Mom's notice.

John found a carpentry-type job at Glenway Supplies, a window factory in Winnipeg. This was only a half-hour drive and soon he found neighbors with whom he could commute.

The very first stage of settling in was done. Things were

going so well that their worrisome fears were pushed into the background and a feeling of thanksgiving filled their hearts. Anna found herself humming old hymns of faith and uttering prayers of praise.

Dear God, we thank you for the hope
That prayers to you so oft evoke.
For peace that lives within our heart
Because you are so great a part.
For hands that share and hearts that sing
And all the blessings life can bring;
For little feet and childish prayers
That wipe away our worldly cares.
Dear God, we thank you on this day
As silently we pause to pray.
We ask your guidance for the way
So hate or fear would never stay.
For love and faith and friendship true
For hands to work and work to do,
Tomorrow's dreams that we have planned,
The beauties of this wondrous land.
For life so rich, for untold joys,
The smiles of little girls and boys,
For such a very goodly part
We thank you, God, with all our heart.

(Garnett Ann Schultz)

To begin a whole new household, a job she had but scarcely begun, was an intriguing project for Anna. Still, there were problems. Arthur had finished first grade in Paraguay, but, in order to get his English, he was now forced to repeat it. As for John and Anna, they learned only enough English to get by. That meant only a few words here and there. They felt most comfortable among friends whom they found quite willing to help out in moments of need. Even when they began to understand and speak more fluently, they did not learn the technical aspects — the reading and writing.

After settling in and getting adjusted to the many unfamiliar aspects of their new lifestyle, John and Anna had a big task before them, that of seeking aid for Anna's health. Visiting a doctor, however, was complicated by the fact that they needed to bring along an interpreter. Pastor and Mrs. Rempel, who had visited them during their first week and invited them to church, soon became instrumental in finding the right doctors, bringing them there and also interpreting for them.

Anna still had frequent severe headaches which blanked out her memory during the onslaught. In order to find the cause, a number of tests were done. This included the E.E.G. test done in Winnipeg, which produced no helpful results. No evidence of a suspected tumor was found.

Suddenly Anna became ill again and was admitted to the Steinbach Hospital. She knew in her heart that it was another malaria relapse, but the doctors were not willing to accept her diagnosis. Blood tests showed that something definitely was wrong. She was transferred to the St. Boniface Hospital, Winnipeg, where she remained for two weeks of intensive tests. Doctors there suspected leukemia but couldn't locate the missing link. Only considerably later did they realize that it must have been the malaria bug still in her system that had stumped them. Malaria, after all, was not a Canadian problem.

After several minor surgeries Anna breathed a sigh of relief, and confidence filled the couple. God had been good and life now seemed brimful of promise. The doctor's latest comments about Anna's malaria (they now believed her to be fully cured) sounded wonderfully good, so good, in fact, that they decided cheerfully to ignore their own contradictory thoughts on the subject and simply believe.

"Let's just thank the Lord for His answer to our prayers, and not worry about anything," Anna suggested. The sparkle was coming back into her eyes again and John knew that was reason enough for him to praise the Lord. To agree with her came easily, and it seemed the most natural thing in the world to bow before God in humble thanksgiving.

The Easter season, their second in Canada, was upon them. Anna was feeling good and revelled in the prospect of the holidays. Back in Paraguay she could never have visualized having John home every night and every weekend. It was as if a fairy godmother had come along to hand out her heart's desire. Now a festive feeling was in the air. And to top it off, John would be home for several days on end. All day! Together they would enjoy the family, together they would sleep in, together they would do whatever came up.

It was early Easter morning. Sleepily Anna turned and looked at the time. Four o'clock. "Wow!" she murmured to herself. "What's the matter with me? *We had planned to sleep in!*" Now she was wide awake. Something had awakened her with a start, but what?

In that quiet hour it came to her like a voice in the night. "It is I. I want to talk to you." Awed, she listened further. "I want you to go back to Bolivia as a missionary." She couldn't believe it! What was she hearing? The thought was so foreign, her mind wanted only to reject it. The voice came again. "I want you to be a missionary for Me in Bolivia." It was clear, so real. She looked around for a person. She trembled. Was this God? It seemed incredible. Didn't He know she was banned, so to speak, from malaria-infested countries? Didn't He know they had six children?

Blurry thoughts tumbled wildly in her mind. She remembered the time she had prayed that God would speak *clearly* if He wanted to tell them something. She remembered the many times she used to wonder about the vague, seemingly meaningless, longings of her heart. Was this now an answer to all that? Or was it just the figment of her imagination?

She lay there trying vainly to piece together a puzzle that wouldn't fit. Suddenly she realized that her husband too had been tossing and turning for some time. She'd been too preoccupied to notice, but now it struck her that he must be awake.

"Aren't you sleeping, dear?" she queried softly.

"No, I can't," he sighed. "I keep getting such strange thoughts."

"Like what?"

"Well, . . . I know you'll say it's weird, but I awakened and had very strong feelings that we should go to Bolivia as missionaries. It was so clear, as if a voice was saying the words audibly. I've been trying to push it away, to ignore it, but it keeps coming back. It stays with me as if it's real."

"John," her voice was hesitant, a little scared. "I . . . er . . . had the same thing happen to me. Exactly the same. I can't believe it. *I can't believe it!*"

After a long, very still moment, John spoke again. "We might as well get up." His voice was strangely deep and husky.

It felt strange sitting on the couch in their living room during the wee hours of the morning. The reason for being there felt even stranger. The rest of the house and the rest of the world seemed terribly quiet, as if God Himself had shut off all other vibrations in order to make Himself heard. Without a word but with mutual feelings, they bowed their heads in silent reverence to the Presence of the One who was speaking.

Minutes ticked by. They sat in silence. Finally John began. "What do you think? What shall we make of this?"

Anna could not immediately think of any answer. Both fell silent again.

After a while they began sharing their feelings. What were the pros and cons? What did all this mean? They had the cultural background; some experience; the basic language — Spanish (especially John) — and, over the years both had experienced frequent, sometimes urgent, 'tugs' inside towards mission work.

Cons: Anna's serious health problem with the Paraguayan doctor's solemn warning; six children that took a lot of care and money; no formal training or Bible education.

In practical terms, the 'call' did not make sense. "Against" items outweighed the "for."

"And yet, . . . and yet," Anna groped for words. "If this is God . . . if this is from God, then doesn't the fact that He says so overrule all our arguments?"

Their unspoken motto had always been, "When you know God's will, you'd better do it." John often had said, "If God said it, so be it." Did they not know what God wanted? Yet the struggle raged, like two vicious creatures fighting, wanting rather to devour each other than to let the other win.

They had settled down long enough to envision a beautiful future for themselves and their family. Financial security was a definite possibility as was the "better health" prospect in this adopted country. There were opportunities for education, social advancement, government 'helps' for almost anything you needed from child care to Medicare to . . . . They could go on and on.

They had just barely sampled these privileges. And now? Now to give them up before they ever had an opportunity to eat the cake, so to say? It seemed foolish. Incredible!

Shortly after arriving in Canada they had felt themselves being lured into a trap of money and possessions. Using Matthew 6:33 as their basis, they had dedicated themselves anew and had vowed not to get ensnared. Now the two voices persisted. Finally, tired of resisting and struggling, John whispered, "Let's pray."

He grabbed her hands and held them tightly in his. Hesitantly, he began, "God, heavenly Father, we're humbled and unworthy to come before You. We cannot really grasp what it means that You have spoken to us this night. But we want to respond, to acknowledge Your call." He paused, not knowing how to continue. Then, "We want to hear Your voice, obey Your orders. We cannot see through, but with Your help we will try . . ." Another pause. "We don't know how Lord, but let us give this problem back to You. When

You want us to make a move, any move to obey You, please let us know. Please, speak to us again. We are willing but we need to know what to do and when to do it. Help us wait for You to show us."

It was out, spoken, committed.

The struggle was over, but so was the desire for any sleep! A feeling of deep peace and a thrill of expectancy flowed through them, as clear, or perhaps clearer, than any they had ever experienced.

Anna's Bible, as she picked it up, opened of its own accord, to just the right place. "They that wait upon the Lord, shall renew their strength, they shall mount up with wings as eagles; they shall run, and not be weary; they shall walk, and not faint" (Isaiah 40:31).

"Hmm, such a promise is almost too good to be true," mused Anna, as she closed her Bible. Her eyes felt a little heavy. She closed them, thinking that maybe she could doze off for a few minutes.

She sensed the brightening sky of a new day. The children would awaken her to the new day, a lovely brand new Easter Day, and . . . perhaps to a whole new life.

"They that wait upon the Lord . . . they that wait . . . upon the . . . Lord . . . shall renew . . . shall . . . renew . . ."

Morning came. John and Anna decided to wait with telling people. When the Lord would show them what to do next, then they'd get on with it and tell the world. And so, even the pastor of their church, the Word of Life Mission, did not know the meaning of the glow on their faces that Easter morning. Nor did anyone else.

Outwardly their lives went on very much as before.

The call stayed with them and affected their lives in hidden ways. Every time a decision had to be made, this call was in the balance. How would the decision fit?

But the next step was not clear. Some days a feeling of frustration set in. "Wasn't it real? Why is nothing happening? What did God want?"

Later the thought struck them that maybe God hadn't meant Bolivia at all. Maybe He just meant for them to serve Him better at home. Surely that must have been what God meant.

"Let's get involved with that nice newly-built German church in town," John ventured. "We know the language so much better. We could help in its various ministries, Sunday school, whatever. Perhaps that was what God had in mind for us all along."

They went, and continued to go for the next two months. But the searched-for assurance never came. Just as the wise men who searched in Jerusalem enroute to Bethlehem, found they had detoured, so John and Anna needed to get back to the path and simply follow the Star — God's will.

The waiting continued. The months changed to a year. One year changed to two. Where was God and His call? Where were His promises?

It was the spring of 1972.

After experiencing some severe physical problems combined with a run-down feeling, Anna had once more gone to see the doctor. This wasn't the first time. Only last fall one doctor had tried to console her with nerve pills. Convinced that this was not her problem, she had refused them. Now, however, she'd decided to wait no longer. Her problem had to be solved. Tests were taken and sent away for analysis.

Anna was busy ironing, when the persistent ring of the telephone interrupted her.

"I would like you and your husband to come in. There are things I need to discuss with you." The voice on the phone sounded pleasant enough, and yet Anna stiffened. She detected an undercurrent of seriousness which frightened her.

"When do you want us to come?"

"Today or tomorrow, as soon as you can, please." The doctor sounded firm. "I have the tests back and need to talk to you about them."

The words echoed and re-echoed in her mind. "He *needs* to talk to me. He *needs* to talk to me." The simple words began to have an ominous sound which taunted her. If only John were home! They could go at once and get it over with. *Get it over with,* for better or for worse! What would it be?

"The tests indicate that you may have cancer." Was he trying to soften the words with that 'maybe'? We will do a hysterectomy at once. We've talked it over with the specialist in the city and made this decision together. That will be the best, the very best we can do."

The verdict was as ominous as the thought had been.

Struggling to accept these words, Anna shuddered involuntarily. Her tears flowed, not in public, but alone on her knees in her tiny blue bedroom. The needs of her little ones were all around her, and their voices clamored for love and attention. How could she leave them, knowing this terrible disease was eating out her insides. Would she return at all? Would she ever be well again? Life certainly played funny tricks. From her side of the picture all seemed in useless jumbles. There was no plan or purpose. Where was God?

She'd had some serious bouts of malaria, alright; the last one in Paraguay had almost killed her. That had been bad, they had thought, but cancer? *Cancer?* The disease that everyone feared and hated, worse than malaria, tuberculosis, epilepsy or even leprosy. Maybe worse than all of those combined! Now she had it. She, Anna Wiens, at the age of thirty-two, had cancer. And to think they had thought God called them to the mission field! Every day, almost, they'd been looking for some signal from Him to indicate it was time for their next step — a step they were prepared to take in faith and obedience. For almost two years they had waited in vain. Nothing, absolutely nothing, was happening. Instead, He was now sending them this — this ugly disease.

"God, where are You, and what is Your plan?" Her deep heart's cry received no answer. Slowly two things helped her. John's love was written clearly on his face these days, and the pain she saw in his eyes somehow helped relieve her own. Secondly, he had made a public prayer request through the church and people were responding to the need. She literally felt the frustration leaving her and being replaced by a new feeling of peace.

"I certainly don't understand the reason for this," she told the nurse, while being prepared for the operating room. "But I'm glad of one thing. I know the One who's in control, and I know that He knows what He's doing, even if I don't."

As Anna was taken into the operating room, the assisting physician suddenly exclaimed, "Hey, *that's bad!* Don't you think maybe we should just forget it? Obviously it's too late."

Dr. Krueger was not inclined to give up. In fact, he was determined to succeed. They would do their very best. Maybe . . .

Did the doctor know, or sense subconsciously, that there were hundreds of people praying for them? And that those earnest petitions would be continued indefinitely? And there was a God at the helm of this family's boat, a God who could control the storm if He wished? Perhaps he knew.

For Anna the valley had only begun. At times she was much too sick to even know it. At other times she felt it and prayed. The penicillin they gave her to fight a threatening infection backfired. Her reaction to it was so violent, it threw her right back on the balances and left her hanging on to life by the slimmest thread.

Hours passed and became days, but the longed-for improvement did not come. The die seemed to be cast. Had the battle been lost before it was started? Was there no chance?

John kept praying. The children prayed most fervently in their own special trusting faith. Many people from far and near were praying, and still she kept losing ground. To the watching, haggard husband, she seemed so hopelessly unconscious. How long was it since she had last responded?

Anna's mind was aroused but nothing was noticeable to those who stood by her. She was in a different world; she didn't know just where, but she was hearing voices. Suddenly one voice, standing out very clearly, was right beside her. "You have been at death's door," it said. "Plans had been made for this to be your end, but I did not allow it. I have put a stop to it, because I love you and need you in My work. My plans for you are all complete. *I have work for you.*"

Anna opened her eyes. She was back in this world and it was John who was beside her, watching and waiting. She didn't know where she had been or how long she had been gone.

A touch of new life seemed to enter her weak body. The nurse became aware of it, and soon the word spread "Anna will make it. *Anna will make it!*"

"Thank you, God." John's voice was hardly audible as unnoticed tears lingered on his eyelids. "Thank you, Lord, for answering our prayers."

Some three days later, Dr. Penner came and sat at her bedside. "Well, Anna," he said reflectively, "You are over the margin now. That was very, very close. Almost, almost, it would have been too late."

VIVID splashes of color on the trees announced the arrival of fall as each brilliantly colored leaf seemed to vie with the other for first place in the Master's art contest. Anna's illness was well in the background. The surgery had been pronounced successful; it was believed that all traces of the cancer had been safely removed.

Rev. Wiebe, their new pastor, met John and Anna one day and seemed very excited. He was doing the groundwork for a missionary conference planned for their church in November. Apparently one of their young people who was attending Prairie Bible Institute had been very impressed with their missionary conference. Now Pastor Wiebe had succeeded in getting the same speaker out to Niverville, and was anticipating a wonderful time.

"By the way," he concluded, "the name of our speaker is Bruce Porterfield. You can join us in prayer for him."

John and Anna were glad no one noticed them at that moment. When that name was mentioned, something like a little bolt of lightning seemed to strike them. Shivers ran up their spines as something told them, "This is it. This is it. This is it!"

It was incredible! Fourteen years ago, when as a young couple they had worked at the New Tribes missionary school, Bruce and Edith Porterfield had been one of the missionary couples with whom they worked. Edith had been like a second mother to Anna, heartily taking her in, accepting her, loving her. Those days had seemed so long ago. Now, suddenly they sprang back to life.

"Anna," John announced the following day. "I feel the Lord is speaking to us. Now is the time that we've been waiting for so long. It is time for us to . . . to take a step of faith, somehow. To make a move."

She felt the same way. "What does that imply? What move do you think we should make?" she queried thoughtfully.

"Well, for one thing, let's tell Pastor Wiebe." He sounded quite decisive.

It was funny to see the surprise on Mr. Wiebe's face when they told him their story. They must be the last couple he'd imagined being called to the mission field, but his initial surprise soon turned to radiance. He listened with the keenest interest.

"It must be the dream of every evangelical pastor to see his people receive and heed the call of God in their lives," he reflected a little later. He encouraged John and Anna; from that night onward they experienced his loving support for that still unknown project.

Their meeting with Bruce at the service was a unique experience. Travelling in an English country, he was totally taken aback when someone heartily greeted him in Spanish — until now their only common language. It took awhile for the facts to register. When Bruce realized who John and Anna were he was overjoyed. To the amazement of everyone else, the three soon were involved in animated conversation. They had so much to talk about!

"You must come to our house," Anna insisted. "We have so much that we'd like to share with you."

The visit was great, like old times. It wasn't long before John brought up the subject so warm on their hearts. They were thrilled and felt greatly rewarded when they found Bruce not only supportive but also more than just a little enthusiastic.

"That's it," John announced to Anna after the visit. He sounded glad. "I've told him we are willing and ready to go if God opens the doors."

Anna wasn't surprised; she'd been listening and taking things in. But in spite of that, the butterflies now suddenly fluttering in her stomach threatened for the moment to destroy her serenity. Was it really true? At last, after all this waiting? Would it work out?

As one gropes for a wall when attacked by a dizzy spell, so her heart now reached out for God and just one extra stamp of His approval. Almost immediately she sensed His presence, and the memory of that verse with which He had spoken to her that special Easter morning flashed through her mind. "They that wait upon the Lord shall renew their strength; they shall mount up with wings as eagles; they shall run and not be weary. . . ."

Anna was comforted and convinced! Nothing would keep her back.

Bruce Porterfield helped them make the application. Would they be accepted? What if they were not? Then what? The waiting seemed unbearable, but finally the news came. They were accepted! New Tribes Mission had accepted them as missionaries in training and enrolled them in Boot Camp in Durham, Ontario. Classes were to begin at the end of January, giving them only weeks to sell, prepare, pack and be gone. Bruce Porterfield was very helpful in working with them to make the necessary arrangements.

The urgency and busyness of the schedule mingled with the excitement of it all. The festive season became very special in a lot of ways.

A friend of Anna's had dropped in for a cup of coffee. Across the kitchen table, with the low winter sun shining genially through the small, curtained window, their conversation flowed freely, warmly. Very soon it turned to the subject so vibrant, and yet so nearly untouched.

"I can't begin to describe how thrilled I am at God's leading," she shared. "It has become so clear, so forceful almost, and direct. For awhile we had so many reasons to doubt and wonder. Sometimes we just felt like giving up in despair, but now we can see it. Just think — *He knew the whole thing all the time!* His promises are so completely reliable."

As she was about to fall asleep that night, Anna recalled the words John had shared after they experienced that Easter morning call. She prayed that she and her family might always remember and live by those words: "When you know God's will you'd better do it. If God said it, so be it." With that being the case — and Anna was firmly convinced that it was — she knew there was no room, no room at all, for doubt.

Chapter Seven

A TROUBLED frown rumpled Anna's delicate brow. Her face flushed. It seemed as though this were the hundredth time she'd run into a dead-end. The words just wouldn't come. It was embarrassing, to say the least. Even the German-English dictionary she constantly carried with her did not help enough. Here in Durham, Ontario, for the first time in their lives, John and Anna lived in an English-only world. This realization, coupled with the fact that they knew less English than they had thought they did, came as a humiliating, discouraging kind of shock.

"If I had realized how terrible I'd feel about the language problem I might never have come," John confided one day.

Anna thought, "If that's the case, I'm glad we didn't know, or God would have never gotten us here."

Today it was her turn to have the blues. Every time she wanted to express her feelings or explain something she got totally frustrated.

"But," she feebly preached encouragement to herself, "we cannot give up. The staff members are being so thoughtful, allowing us to write all our assignments phonetically if we like. The fellow students like John and Mary Tibberts, Elmer and Tina Barkman, the Jim Loewens and others are so helpful so many times. I know some day we're going to get it. *We've got to!*"

At the end of the first month John Tibbert announced, "I want to go to Owen Sound and get each of you an English Bible. Want to come along?"

To own their first English Bible, was thrilling, although their first attempts at reading were anything but beautiful. The stuttering and stammering couldn't dampen their feelings of satisfaction. Stubbornly and faithfully they kept at it and

71

very shortly their German Bibles were tucked away in drawers. Some day these Bibles would make good souvenirs.

During their fourth month in Durham, both John and Anna realized that something special was happening to them. They had taken no English courses. Now, suddenly, their problem was gone. They could read, write, understand and communicate in English. A miracle had happened, not in a moment, but in four months. The greatness of God overwhelmed them as fervent whispers of "thank you, Lord, thank you, Lord," were heard several times from both of them before the still hush of the night overtook them.

Anna was now able to concentrate on other things. She became aware of a deep inner peace, deeper perhaps than any she'd experienced before. The sense of fulfillment filled her with joy which bubbled over in all sorts of nice little ways.

Just to behold Anna's happy face was a pleasure. So many times in the past she had tried to resign herself to the fact that she was only a mother. Housework too often had been more of a drudgery than she wanted to admit. Always there was somewhere in the back of her mind an unnamed desire — a longing she could not quite define but that seemed to hold her back from fully enjoying herself. Now that aching something was gone, and she was at peace with herself.

The study of God's word opened up whole new avenues for both John and Anna. The English Bible seemed to say things in such new and different ways. At times it seemed like a book they'd never read before! They drank it all in with the heartiness of "hungering and thirsting after righteousness," as described in Matthew chapter five.

Another spiritual adventure was the prospect of simply learning to walk with God. The more they experimented the more exciting it became. To tell Jesus every frustration, to ask Him about every question, to have Him guide in every decision, to trust Him with every problem. Wow! Then the Christian life had potential and meaning — a deep kind of meaning that too often they'd missed before; a meaning that provided answers.

BETWEEN the first and second semester came the Jungle Camp. This six-week camp-out in the bush was compulsory for all missionary candidates, and proved to be an exciting, preparatory adventure. It was direct, specific, training for real jungle life.

About a mile behind the school yard the candidates built huts out of unfinished logs. The roof and part of the walls were finished with plastic. The beds were made of poles, with woven strings for a mattress. Room partitions were made of either plastic or blankets.

An outhouse was under one tree, with plastic attached around it to provide privacy. The shower, under another tree, consisted of a pail of water hung from a branch, with nailpunched holes at the bottom. The water was carried from the nearby brook. Whoever wanted a shower had to remember to undress before he "turned on" the shower. It went to work rather promptly! The shower too was closed off for privacy with a sheet of plastic. Since these 'conveniences' were used by several families, they used a little flag at the "door" or opening to insure privacy. Up meant "it's busy."

Families were not allowed to go shopping more than the few designated times. When they could go, they went on foot and backpacked the groceries home. There was little time for frivolities.

The time spent in the "jungle," however, was packed full of numerous exciting extras. Every man, woman, and child had to know how to swim. The nearby lake afforded a convenient place for daily lessons. It didn't take Anna long to learn. For her this was a novel experience on which her adventure-loving spirit thrived. She especially appreciated this time that seemed cut out just right for playing and laughing with her own rapidly growing-up family. She realized that this always needed to be an important part of her plans.

All the men and women learned to cut their spouse's hair.

(What jungle offers hairdressers?) Anna did not need to participate in the chicken butchering lessons because she knew that art well from experience. Every 'unskilled' woman learned the art of cathcing, killing, eviscerating, and preparing a chicken from start to finish. She did, however, take part in the shooting exercises, a very new experience. Both pistols and shotguns were used. Everyone, including the most timid woman, had to practice and master the art of being a reasonably accurate and confident marksman. A missionary wife in a real jungle situation needed to be able to survive even if her husband were missing and there were no food in the house.

One unforgettable event of these weeks was a hike down Bruce Trail between Niagara Falls and Owen Sound. All the women of the jungle camp participated. They left their husbands and children at home to have special batching practice. The wives had not been allowed to prepare any food in advance.

The women walked twelve unfamiliar miles the first day, backpacking all their food, bedding, tents and cooking utensils. Only the staff members were acquainted with their route. On the second morning the women were forced to play a game of soccer, of all things, to ease away the soreness before beginning the next trek.

On the last lap of this second and final day, Anna saw some of her friends strangely stagger and sway. Her natural empathy aroused, she wanted to help but found herself suddenly unable. She too was totally exhausted. Although the strain was tremendous, everyone made it home before succumbing to utter exhaustion. After a brief rest, Anna asked herself, "How soon will this be real? How soon will we need this kind of guts and perseverance in our everyday life, trekking down steaming jungle trails and never quite knowing where we are?"

THE second semester began with a flourish. How time

had flown! With the language barrier overcome, Anna now dove into her studies with all possible enthusiasm. The study load included Bible study courses in the mornings, and a work detail in the afternoons. Anna and the other mothers were exempted from the work detail. Anna used this time for the house and family.

A visiting friend asked her one day, "How do you really like it here?"

Her answer was warm and spontaneous. "Why, I love every minute of it! I like the simple lifestyle, the different atmosphere, but what I like the most is the spiritual aspect. It's hard to believe how I've changed."

A misty, faraway look clouded her brown eyes for a moment. Almost wistfully she continued, "Sometimes I see myself again as I was when I first accepted Jesus into my heart and life. An immature teenager, struggling under an extreme emotional strain, I gave myself to God, with nothing, absolutely nothing, to offer Him. Then He began, bit by bit, to change me according to His plans."

"How do you mean?"

"Well, it's like this. I had learned nothing back then about consciously trusting on a daily basis. Nothing about asking His guidance, nothing about claiming His promises. In a vague sort of way I counted on God to help me, but it was always I who needed to be strong and tough, who needed to do things in my own strength. And yet I wasn't strong. I stumbled all the time. Sometimes I think I must have been much like Peter, outwardly happy-go-lucky, always lively, eager, outspoken, making quick and often foolish decisions, but inwardly where people couldn't see, I had very intense feelings, strong passionate desires and idealistic aspirations. When I think of Peter I'm comforted to think God chose such an imperfect one to be one of Jesus' chosen twelve. The very thought gives me hope."

"But now you say all this has changed for you?"

"Yes and no. Yes, because I really believe I'm different.

I have learned so much. Each event, even when it seemed *terrible* at the time, served a purpose and helped me grow. It was much like climbing a ladder, one rung at a time. From my present vantage point, the whole experience of the Christian life seems a perfectly wonderful thing. And I know I'm not the same person I used to be.

"On the other hand, though, I know I haven't arrived. The Lord has *many* more rungs for me to climb . . . the last rung will take me to heaven," Anna concluded softly, reverently.

The two went their separate ways, one reflecting thoughtfully on the strangely deep turn in the conversation and wondering how her own spiritual life could become more vibrant. The other, Anna, noting with joy her happy circumstances. Her feet seemed light, her whole body young, agile and free.

"God is so good," she whispered fervently to herself. Little did she guess that in the months and years ahead, there would be even harder rungs; yes, impossible rungs to climb, and that she would almost lose that vision.

Almost before they knew it the eleven months at Durham were finished. They had graduated and were ready for the next stage. After spending about a month during Christmas holidays with loved ones in Manitoba, they were off to language school at Camdenton, Missouri.

Here they were challenged with a whole new set of courses, courses that spoke of an urgency, of a soon-to-be-upon-them need that required immediate preparation. Their work revolved around five main courses.

One was *Phonetics,* the study of sounds in order that these strange sounds can be written down phonetically so as to make a suitable alphabet, spelling rules, everything, to bring these new sounds, not only to comprehension in your own mind, but to a readable language on paper.

Secondly, there was *Field Medicine.* "That was my favorite subject right from the beginning," Anna declared.

Visiting doctors as well as their own doctor taught the course. It included many things ordinary lay people would never have been told; taking care of yourself in adverse conditions, diagnosing disease, giving medication and needles (they practiced those on each other), stitching up wounds and delivering a baby, were only some of the vast number of things to learn. How to cope with emergencies, all types, was another extremely important aspect. This "how-to" list included treatment for shock, fainting, snake and insect bites, as well as pointers on what to do when someone's heart suddenly stopped beating.

They learned to think, "If only one co-worker and I were out in the jungle and something happened to him, what would I do?" To be knowledgeable and prepared, they were told, was more than half the answer in any emergency.

Anna often thought, "Wow, this is exciting! I wish I could go now. I wish I could just go in somewhere among needy, needy people and 'doctor' my heart out to them. This subject is something I *really* want to put to use."

The third subject, *Bible Translation,* dealt with learning the techniques of careful, accurate translation of God's word into previously unknown languages.

Fourth, was *Language Study,* related to the field to which workers would be sent. Spanish was their language, and even John, who was fluent in it, found many new things to learn. To Anna, who had stumbled along with only the most necessary words and phrases, it was a whole new chapter and a giant-sized task.

Fifth, was the challenging *Culture Study.* White people in America tend to think of colored people as the strangers and foreigners — outsiders. Now the missionary, became the foreigner, and the long task of learning to understand and accept the culture of a strange people needed to be learned. To Anna, the many different cultures, with difficult verbal communication, made each assignment look awesome.

"This subject has really intrigued me," John confided to

Anna one night. She could tell by the look on his face that he was really into it. This was his thing. In her mind's eye she could envision him, searching out the unreached people in foreign jungles, and finding ways to communicate, to learn their culture, to help them. Would it happen? Soon perhaps? She prayed that night for John especially, that the longing of his heart might be fulfilled.

TOWARDS the end of the last semester, a cloud emerged quite suddenly on Anna's horizon and simply hung there. A cloud of gloom and dread, a cloud of terrible conflict. It wasn't the first time such a thing had happened (could she ever forget?) but this time it especially grabbed her as if she were a little object in a giant vise. The more she tried to suppress it the worse it got. She became miserably disgusted with herself. One would have thought, she reasoned, that with the way she'd been maturing spiritually during the last few years, such a thing would not happen again. She struggled even harder with the apparently shameful fact that she struggled! It became one vicious circle.

She knew the right verses and tried vainly to preach them to her own soul. "My grace is sufficient for thee: for my strength is made perfect in weakness. Most gladly therefore will I glory in my infirmities, that the power of Christ may rest upon me" (II Cor. 12:9).

The needed response refused to come. A dark wall remained before her. There simply was no way around it, over it or beside it. Grimly, as if possessing a demon of its own, the darkness spoke to her. "It's almost time now. You will have to give up your children. You will have to give up all of your children."

She had known all along that going to the tribes would mean leaving the children at the mission school for long periods of time. Now, however, it seemed that Satan himself had wedged his way in and was having her face things his way. And she could not — she simply could not give up her children! No way was she prepared to give up her children for the sake of some dirty, ignorant natives, *savages perhaps!* From a distance the problem hadn't loomed so large, but now it was gigantic, and she knew that unless she became willing, totally willing, at a close range, she would become a drop-out, a quitter before she ever got started. Oh, why was the struggle so hopelessly hard? Surely she had thought too soon that God had helped her grow strong. She must have been presumptuous, wrong.

Hours of secret weeping at night became common. The truth of Ephesians 6:12 became more evident, "For we wrestle not against flesh and blood, but against principalities, against powers, against the rulers of the darkness of this world. . . ."

Jean Johnson noticed her now frequently tear-stained face, her deep agitation. "Come over tonight for a nice little visit," Jean urged one afternoon.

Anna didn't need much time to make up her mind. She had to talk to someone.

Jean was so understanding — her insight and empathy drew the words right out of Anna, and her gentle but decisive counsel had a very positive effect. The poem she gave Anna had a special message just for her.

Don't Quit
When the mountain looks high,
And the valley is far too low,
It's not time to quit,
It's only time to go.
 When life's battle is rough
 And you can't seem to win,
 It's not time to quit,
 It's time to begin.
When your friends let you down,
You don't know where to turn,
It's not time to quit
It's time to stand firm.

When your witness seems nil
And your spirit's sunk low,
It's not time to quit,
You must get up and go.
When your world is in turmoil
And unbelief sweeps through the land,
It's not time to quit,
It's time to take a stand.
When you look at others
Who do nothing but sit,
You still must keep going,
It's *not* time to quit,
Jesus kept going to Calvary,
He never backed up a bit,
He kept right on — till He died for us.
What if *He* had quit?

Anna knew that she must bring this frustration to a conclusion. During the stillness of the night she stared up at the colorless ceiling. "I have to do something — and do it now!" she moaned. "I need to make a complete dedication to God, a completely new dedication. Why does it have to come to this? Am I not totally committed? Is this what Paul meant when he said, 'I die daily'? Did he have to make many re-dedications? Do I have to commit myself to God again, and again?"

The battle raged inside. She tossed and turned. She felt like screaming! She cried uncontrollably. She had given up trying to stifle the sobs that now tore at her body. "Why was God doing this to her? What was to happen?" she kept asking over and over.

Gradually the storm subsided. She could not tell how much later, but finally the storm was spent. Was that a little voice she was now hearing? Was someone talking to her?

"Remember when you prayed to me in Paraguay? You wanted to live long enough to see your children saved? I have answered that prayer, haven't I?"

Yes, that was true. A vision of her children appeared before her eyes. Arthur and Albert, both so rapidly growing taller and manlier. Rachel — was it only yesterday when Anna had marvelled at her winsome attitude and developing loveliness? Veronica and Monica — with their impish little grins, equally sweet and cunning — were a special bundle of their own. And Freddie, her baby, teasing, mischievous and certainly not a baby any longer. . . . Yes, each of them had personally prayed, asking Jesus into his heart and life. And she, Anna, had been quite closely involved in the making of those decisions.

A feeling akin to shame filled her. Then the voice came again, and she listened with even keener attention. "How many times have I answered your prayers? How often have I been patient with you when you struggled with doubts and questions? How many times have you literally been at death's door and I healed you miraculously? Don't you see that I've had a purpose in all these things? *I now want you,* all of *you.* Is that too much to ask?"

Her resistance melted. "No, Lord, *no, Lord,* it's not too much. Suddenly her response became positive, "Yes, Lord, I'll give myself to you, all the way. Everything, even the children."

The tears, still flowing freely, now spoke of penitence and commitment. They seemed to cleanse and refresh her. What if Christ had not given His all for her?

"Oh Lord," she sighed deeply, for her relief felt so great, "you are so precious and caring. You gave your all. I want to do the same."

The excitement of this new victory could not be contained. She got up, rushed out to where John was still studying, and blurted out the news of her victory. John too was ecstatic, for he had been aware of the undercurrents of struggle in Anna but had been unable to bring it out into the open. Now she had overcome! Together they rejoiced and prayed. Their prayers, and the prayers of countless others were answered that night.

The next morning, as she went to class, the radiance on her face hid the traces of the tear-filled night, but could not hide the excitement of the victory. Jean saw it immediately, squeezed Anna's hand and whispered gently, ''God is good, isn't he?''

John, Anna and family ready to leave on the 12,000 mile trip with their new camperized truck

The Wiens family, just prior to their furlough in 1979. From left to right, Freddie, Monica, Veronica, Anna, Rachel, Arthur, Albert and John

John and Anna, 1980, ready to return to the jungle

John showing off his 'coronation' headgear after he was crowned 'Chief'

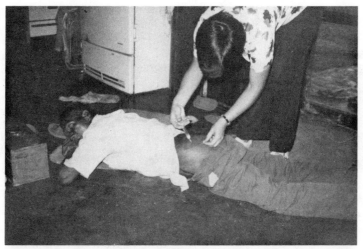

Frequently Anna gave a needle while the patient lay on the floor. This was a difficult position for anyone with back pains

Anna enjoying one of the little ones

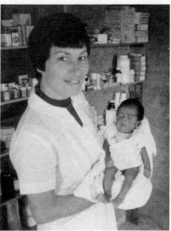

Anna seeking out some medications for one of the babies

Several Ayoré in front of a typical home

John and Anna in the midst of the Ayoré believers, standing in front of their much needed church building

A railway bridge was used to cross a river

The road is never very good, but when the rains come, it becomes virtually impossible

Another view of the mud and water that is called a road

Chapter Eight

WITH the formal part of their training now behind them, John and Anna came back to Manitoba to begin another exciting, still unexplored chapter of their lives. The nitty-gritty of actually getting ready to go was both frightening and delightful.

Classes had ended in January, 1975. Late spring or early summer became their planned time of departure. Those intermissive months were soon filled to the brim with prayer and waiting on the Lord, with planning and church presentations, with physical and material preparations, and with packing for the trip. They anticipated a five year term.

Anna planned wardrobes for their six children. After some consideration she abandoned her original aim of providing a five year supply for each. Not only were funds low, but how could she really tell just how fast each child would grow. Friends and ladies' aid groups from local churches came to her assistance, so that between her own sewing and their timely help, the pile of ready-to-take clothes grew appreciably.

One major item on John's mind, the need of a suitable vehicle, became first an urgent family prayer request, and then a monument of faith as they witnessed God's answers. John and Anna prayed about it many times; then John would go to follow up leads and gain the needed information.

Although the piercing winds chilled him to the bones, John worked outside, not allowing the typical pre-spring Manitoba weather to daunt his enthusiasm. Barely had he warmed up in Anna's cozy kitchen, when he announced decisively, "I'm ready to go ahead now. I feel it's God's time for me to make a purchase. I'm visualizing a Ford truck, a heavy duty one to take the wear and tear of jungle life. It

should be a Crew Cab with its four-door, two-seat conve-
nience to accommodate our family."

With no account to draw from and next to no money in
his pocket he went to see the J.R. Friesen Garage in Steinbach.
To his joy, the salesman was a Christian who heard him out
with good interest. Questions were batted back and forth in
quick succession. The salesman would need a little time to
think. The more than $5000.00 order sounded large when he
had no idea from where the money would come.

After some hesitation, the salesman came up with a unique answer. "We always expect a fair down payment at the
time of the order and we always demand some sort of
guarantee of full payment later. Only people with good jobs
or a reliable source of income can order new vehicles — that's
simply standard procedure. But," he seemed to be measuring
each word carefully, "I am going to do something our company has *never* done before. I will order the truck, exactly as
you have requested it. You give me the down payment when
you can. We will order that truck by faith . . .," he repeated.
"I am excitedly waiting to see just how God will work this
out."

Amazed, John went home, praising the Lord all the way.
At the moment it seemed unreal how good God was. He kept
repeating to himself the precious conviction that God would
undertake. "He will. I know He will."

Two weeks later John was able to bring in a small down
payment. With joy he handed two hundred dollars to the
salesman, and noticed a unique, thoughtful nod accompanying the thank you. "The two of us are in this adventure
together," John thought instinctively. "I wonder who is more
eager to see that it all works out."

John's exercise of faith was really being tested. God had
laid it on his heart not to beg or hint or even make polite
'spiritual' requests for this money. God would provide. Questions of how and when began to plague his mind but with
fresh zeal he refused to doubt. His decision was firm. He must

not and he would not doubt!

The new truck arrived in Steinbach at the due date. Exporting laws demanded that after the official purchase date of the vehicle, it had to leave the country within a month. Therefore this purchase date was postponed until the Wienses departure date could be finalized.

June 2, 1975 was set as their big final day.

"Hey, Dad, do you have the money?" Arthur would ask repeatedly, only to be joined by a chorus of voices.

"How much do we have?"

"Only two weeks to go, Dad. Do you still think it will work out?"

"Of course it will, (stupid)! God always keeps His promises," admonished a younger innocent observer.

"Only ten days left! I heard Mom say they didn't have half of it yet. She didn't know I could hear, or she'd never have said it."

"Maybe we should pray instead of worry and talk."

"Yeah, you know what? I'll tie a string around my little finger to remind me."

THE second of June arrived! The big day had come. John got out his account book, papers and wallet, as Anna brought the last batch of mail. He counted up the gifts received. "One thousand, two thousand, three thousand, four thousand, five . . . Wow!" he almost shouted it. "Anna, come and look! There is *exactly* as much money as the truck bill."

John phoned their pastor and blurted out, "It's all here! The money is all here for the truck. I'll pick up the truck tomorrow."

The pastor broke down and wept, he muttered a few words and then hung up the phone. He tearfully, but joyfully shook his head. He really had not believed it would happen.

"I knew it would happen," piped up a young voice at the kitchen table. "God told me it would," was her self-conscious, almost inaudible explanation.

Where had the money come from? There were many return addresses; some were from churches, many were from individuals. A lot of checks seemed small and insignificant, but they added up. Where did the money come from? There was no doubt in anyone's mind. That money came from God!

"My God shall supply all your need according to his riches in glory by Christ Jesus" (Phil. 4:19). That verse, hanging on the living room wall, now became a precious living reality. "Isn't it great?" exclaimed one of the boys as he read it again. "God sure keeps His promises."

It was a pleasure to see the salesman's face light up with joy and perhaps a fair amount of relief when the transaction was completed. Maybe, just maybe, he'd try that again sometime.

John became a busy carpenter during those next days as he built a sleeper-camper onto the truck. John and Anna would sleep over the cab, two children would sleep on the truck seats while four others would sleep on the two sets of bunks in the back. Sliding windows in both cab and camper faciliated easy slipping back and forth of the children. This would be a help on the twelve thousand-mile trip ahead of them. (Winding roads through the Andes mountains accounted for some of those extra miles.) The camp-style stove and table would, together with prepared food items, provide them with a lot of eating out possibilities.

Young Freddie had nothing better to do than to crawl in and out of the half finished camper. Of course, he was helping like his big brothers were. Somehow it was overlooked when he spilled nails or lost tools. No one seemed to mind, for they were having a lot of fun together.

The trailer to haul their heavy extra luggage and supplies had been built beforehand and was now ready for loading. The time of departure was very close. It seemed that all things were now ready. . . .

Yet in one way — one very major way — John and Anna were not ready to go. They had received no word from mission headquarters as to their exact job location. Could they go without that? From the start, whenever they had prayed that God would lead them to the right spot in Bolivia, it had seemed so reasonable that they should work with the Quechua people, descendants of the Incas. This was a large tribe, very needy but quite civilized. This would be a reasonably safe place to work. John and Anna had felt a burden for these people. The only problem was that this was *their* thinking. They had received no indication of God's plan in the matter. Was it right to proceed along with their own desire or should they keep waiting for further directions?

Finally a letter arrived from the field committee in Bolivia, asking them to come and work with the Ayoré.

"No! This can't be! It just can't be," gasped Anna.

Shudders of deep anguish, almost shock, throbbed through both of them. Neither John nor Anna had wanted to work with this tribe, although they had to admit they were most familiar with this tribe. The Ayoré were a very hostile, rough, still largely uncivilized people. Stories of outright killings and premediated murder among them and by them were rampant. While at boot camp in Durham the reading of **God Planted Five Seeds** had been compulsory. Never would they forget the story of those five missionaries killed in their first attempt to befriend the then totally unknown Ayoré. *Were these people now to become their people?*

Although a lot of progress had been made in the work among this tribe, John and Anna knew that it had been slow and sometimes most unrewarding. There were still many unreached villages or wandering groups left — groups who had never seen a white man or had any encounter with civilization; groups that were as wild and barbaric as ever. As they earnestly considered and prayed, John and Anna became more convinced that this was indeed's God's voice telling them His plan.

Dangerous or not, pleasant or unpleasant, this must be God's will. Their motto, "When you know God's will, you'd better do it," burned itself into their minds. With this new realization and surrender their dread disappeared and was replaced by keen anticipation. Even their youthful encounters with the Paraguayan Indians now became something to appreciate, like an anchor for a boat or a bright spot on an otherwise uncharted future.

Anna paused. The work was so nearly done, she ought to continue. John and the boys were out on the yard, strapping down the final boxes. Soon the trailer would be ready to go. She could see them all clearly through the window. Sweat and grime showed on her husband's brow, as well as on the boys', but that, as usual, only thrilled her. It reminded her of their happy enthusiasm and rugged determination.

But Anna was tired. She needed a break. With a sigh she plunked herself into one of the few remaining chairs. Wearily she closed her eyes. "Only for a few minutes," she mused, and wondered if that would relieve the swirling mud-pool feeling in her forehead, or the dull, tired ache in her back?

In. Out. In. Out. She breathed deeply, regularly for a few minutes. The tension and weariness began to slip away a little and she could think more clearly. These last weeks had not been easy. All the sewing, planning, shopping and packing had been a big job. So had their deputation duties, the visiting of various groups, individuals and churches to present their anticipated work and receive, hopefully, good prayer support as well as at least a fair percent of the recommended support money. This latter aspect of the job had not particularly appealed to either John or Anna, and just thinking of it now made Anna feel tired all over again. Much, much rather would they go with half support than resort to begging or even asking politely. And yet a family of eight needed money.

Was this a struggle peculiar to them or did all missionaries go through this? Was it only a phase, or would such things always be with them?

Shifting her position a bit she sighed, "I guess this is what God wants me to keep learning, all over again every day. To simply trust Him with all my needs. All the children's needs. Yes . . . simply trust Him . . ."

The door banged suddenly and the sound of scurrying, boyish feet bade her get up quickly. "We're done, Mom," fairly yelled Albert. "All done."

John came along more slowly; his steps seemed measured and thoughtful, but his smile warmed Anna's heart. Cheerfully she got out a jug of juice and the half-empty cookie jar. Her crew deserved some refreshments and she wasn't about to let them down.

Half an hour later she was ready to resume her own duties. She realized suddenly that her headache and backache were gone, and she hadn't even prayed about it. God was so good, and she so unworthy.

Her special verse came back to her. She hadn't had it on her mind for a while, so now it seemed all fresh and new. "They that wait upon the Lord shall renew their strength, they shall mount up with wings as eagles. . . ."

The praise in her heart needed an outlet, and soon she burst out heartily singing an old-fashioned hymn. On John's way out, he showed his approval by pecking her lightly and planting a quick kiss on her cheek before disappearing out the door. His quickness allowed her just enough time to give him a light poke in the ribs.

Chuckling slightly, Anna spoke aloud to herself, "Life is good. Really good. Even for a missionary family getting ready to go on a long, long trip without all the money people say they should have." It didn't matter that Rachel had heard and was watching her gravely now, her big blue eyes wide open. Anna merely bent over and gave her an extra squeeze, feeling a deep bond of love welling up in her heart.

"God, keep my precious children," she breathed, silently now. "Please God."

THE all-important journey began early Monday morning. The days, at first quite uneventful, held many humdrum hours of weary travelling. Occasionally events occurred to help liven them up. After getting into Mexico, excitement became an almost constant companion. But they continued on into Guatemala.

"When are we ever going to stop for a break?" came a whining voice from the back. "Our clothes are all sticky from sweat."

"Right, pretty soon we're going to stink," someone agreed without hesitation.

They finally decided to stop for some relaxation on Saturday in El Salvador where they found a nice air-conditioned hotel. That, and a shower helped relieve the unbearable heat. They phoned home to Niverville with an "all is well" message.

After a brief half-day off in El Salvador, they pressed on again through Honduras and Nicaragua, where they saw much evidence of the shambles and terror created by an earthquake. Then it was on to Costa Rica which, after all the Spanish countries, seemed attractive with its English.

At the Costa Rican border a pleasant looking young man, claiming to be a pilot, approached them requesting a ride. John and Anna had been warned repeatedly not to pick up any hitchhikers so John asked the border personnel whether they knew the young man. Was he trustworthy? Receiving affirmative answers he decided to try it. The hitchhiker turned out to be a blessing. After enjoying very pleasant conversation they arrived in his home town, San José, where he insisted that they stop at his house. Both he and his mother were eager to reward John and Anna for the ride and so the whole family ended up staying for the night. The little seemingly insignificant country had indeed turned out to be an oasis in their desert.

In Panama a new course lay before them. Their truck needed to be shipped by cargo to Guayaquil, Ecuador. During the waiting period in Panama the family visited a couple from their home church in Niverville. This couple gave them a tour of the HCJB Spanish-English radio station. After allowing two weeks for the truck to reach Ecuador, the Wiens family flew to Quito and then continued to Guayaquil by bus. Here they were told that the truck, which they had expected to be ready, could only be released after the weekend. They found a hotel for this waiting period.

Such waiting was tiring. Would that from now on always be included in their daily schedule? They wondered. During the last number of years they had forgotten that many of the southern countries were famous for just that. The reflective mood, however, was cut short when Albert came dashing into the room, "Hey, Dad, there's a family down the hall who speak German. They look awfully sad, as if maybe they're lost or something."

John went to investigate and found it just as he'd been told. After listening awhile, he pieced their story together. It was a Mennonite family from Mexico, with thirteen children of all ages, that was stranded there. Although their plane tickets clearly gave Santa Cruz as their destination, airplane personnel had made them stay in Guayaquil, and refused them re-entrance when they attempted to travel on. At their own expense they'd been staying at the hotel and waiting — they didn't know for what. By this time they had run out of both food and money, their baggage was confiscated at the customs, and they could speak not a word of Spanish to communicate their need.

"Wow," John exclaimed, "I didn't know why we had to wait these extra days, but it must have been meant for us to find this family. They are so absolutely helpless and destitute, I can't imagine what they'd do if no one came to help them."

He was roused and ready for action. Determinedly he went to the office at the airport and began to investigate. What was going on? And why? The girl at the desk mistook him for the American ambassador, called the manager and introduced him as such before even giving him a chance to explain. Within minutes, it seemed, the whole mix-up was straightened out. The manager apologized profusely. On Sunday morning the family, after expressing deep gratitude, was on their way to their rightful destination.

"It's a blessing to know more languages, isn't it?" John mused aloud.

"But it's funny that they took you for the American ambassador, isn't it?" piped up Arthur. Ripples of laughter followed his comment, but John was inclined to be serious. "God uses even the mistakes of people. If I'd had a chance to introduce myself first, I might never have gotten anywhere. God used that mistake to stir those people into action."

On the thirteenth of July, John and Anna arrived safely in Cochabamba, Bolivia, right in the heart of South America. They'd been on the road for six weeks. Not once had they been lost or even taken a wrong road. With hearty thanks they praised God, then got to the business of getting a good scrubbing. Were they ever ready for a good bath!

They needed to take the trailer to Tambo, the missionary children's school. The mere sight of the school stirred up special memories for Anna. She saw herself again as the young mother of their firstborn, sick, lonely and depressed. She recalled their last goodbyes to a reluctant staff and remembered the joy of going home to her parents. Who would have guessed she'd be back? Who would have thought they'd bring their kids here where they'd once cared for others' and then given up the venture in disheartening failure?

There wasn't much time to reminisce though. Not right now. The time had come for the next item on their agenda — the bonus Anna had been dreaming of! They were off to Paraguay to visit her parents whom they hadn't seen for seven years. The children were bubbling over with excitement and eagerness. Would they recognize Grandma and Grandpa?

Their welcome home was warm and hearty. To the

children everything seemed very new. They had forgotten so much in seven years. But how they liked it! Why, this was where Mommy grew up and experienced all those exciting things she'd always talked about. And they felt so much love, sweet Christian love.

The three-week visit gave Anna the feeling of having been elevated onto a plateau where she could get a bird's eye view of her life. She simply could rest and enjoy both a backward look and a forward one. Like Jacob of old who had taken his pillow of stone, erected and consecrated it as a monument to God, she too could take all her memories and quietly erect and dedicate them to God. Clearly she could see the picture. Every one of the mysteries and frustrations now had a meaning.

Taking a quiet walk one day, her whole life story began reeling off before her eyes. She saw again the dusty trails and endless rows of corn. She felt again the throbbing aches from long days of cotton picking. She experienced again the one-dress no-shoe wardrobe she'd been so familiar with, sometimes with smoldering resentment, and thrilled all over again at the beautiful newness of a long-awaited pair of shoes.

Today she could see the picture from the upper side. At that time she had seen mostly the knots and tangles, like the underside of a piece of embroidery. No one had told her that God was a master designer and knew the end from the beginning. Maybe she wouldn't have understood if someone had. Looking back now she could see a purpose behind everything. Even the one-dress wardrobe equipped her now to cope well with a meager allowance. Complaints had no room in her thankful mind.

Slowly she turned to today. Would the problems of today eventually reveal their purpose too? Would their mysteries be solved in the answers of her tomorrows?

"I will lift up mine eyes," seemed to beckon her gaze even higher. Words could not describe the assurance that filled her. "God knows me. God plans for me. God loves me,"

93

reverberated through her mind. "It's true. All my tomorrows are in His hand, and everything will turn out right."

It was hard to grasp that God had revealed Himself so personally to her, after her years of searching, of wishing and of waiting. In awe she marvelled at the wonder of it, and realized afresh how very trustworthy He was. It didn't matter that the map of their future was hazy and without roadsigns. It was enough that they'd been given one arrow saying, "Follow Me."

BACK at Tambo, settling in the six children at the various departments of the school was a job in itself. Freddie, the youngest, was inclined to hang on to Mommy. That didn't exactly help. "God, I'm counting on You. You'll just have to help me," she'd whisper resolutely.

Like so many times in the past, John rounded up the family for an evening chat and devotions. The children had changed schools many times and knew what to expect but the prospect of being separated from Mom and Dad for four months at a time was a new and bitter thing to accept. Yet there was no question in any of their minds. This thing was from God and there was no room for rebellion. There couldn't be.

John opened his Bible and read the portion that was by now well known to all of them. Never before had it been so full of meaning though. "Jesus answered and said, 'Verily I say unto you, There is no man that has left house, or brethren or sisters, or father or mother, or wife or children, or lands for my sake and for the gospel's but he shall receive an hundredfold now in this time houses and brethren and sisters and mothers and children and lands with persecutions; and in the world to come eternal life'." (Mark 10:29,30).

They joined hands in a final prayer circle. Tears mingled freely with the simple prayers in that room, but the presence of God was felt in a very real way. Daddy committed each one to God, and each to each other to love, care and support as the needs would arise.

That night Anna took a little extra time falling asleep. Uppermost on her mind, however, were not thoughts of depression or gloom but rather thoughts of victory. "Why, this isn't nearly as bad as Satan used to tell me. What a liar the devil is. . . . And how kind and faithful God is. When we try to reason out our own answers we always get stuck. When we simply trust God, He always supplies. He will supply for our children too."

"So He giveth His beloved sleep" (Psalm 127:2).

At nine o'clock in the morning John and Anna were on the truck, ready to leave. The children, standing around, were smiling through tears. The last goodbyes had been said, the last kisses blown.

They were off.

Just before they turned that final curve heading toward the mountain before them, Anna turned once more to wave. The children too were waiting, straining for the final glimpse. . . .

The ordeal was over. Anna wiped away the tears and turned to John. "Now we have our future to look at. I wonder what lies ahead of us. But then perhaps I shouldn't be wondering, should I? God knows."

"Yes, God knows." His voice was strangely husky. To himself he continued, "And thank you, God for helping us . . . for giving Anna this kind of strength."

Chapter Nine

SHARP edges of apprehension subtly stole into Anna's
heart. She looked at John. The intense concentration he needed
to maneuver the truck through knee-deep ruts and countless
mudholes successfully blocked off any other emotions he
might be feeling.

The sun had set and darkness enveloped them rapidly. The
seven hours on the road had drained Anna of the zest she felt
in the morning. Would they ever get there? And what would
they find?

After spending the night at Santa Cruz, where they had
loaded their truck with a month's supplies, they had set off for
Puesto Paz, the chosen home base for their field of service.
The road, totally unknown to them and very poorly marked,
was unfinished and wound through dense jungle with no
signs of civilization in any direction. The fact that the ground
was saturated by recent rains made the picture even more
dismal, especially after they had found that getting stuck and
working your own way out was to be the norm of the day.

The brief prayers uttered frequently during the day
became longer and more intense as the night approached. By
the time it was completely dark, Anna's prayers had become
unceasing.

Suddenly they heard a commotion and saw strange
movements ahead in the beams of their headlights. Before
they could grasp the situation they were forced to stop. Their
path was entirely blocked by a crowd of partially dressed,
very excited natives. Strange babbling noises interrupted by
laughter and shouting permeated the air. The crowd, arms
waving excitedly, rushed around the truck. Surrounding the
truck, the group felt its smoothness, and then tried the doors.
Some managed to open them and shortly pulled both John and

Anna out of the cab.

What was this? It felt like an attack, but surely it couldn't be! What was the meaning of this? Could it be . . .? Yes, it must be . . . must be a welcoming party! If so, this should be Puesto Paz. But where was the village, and where was the missionary who was to meet them? Something didn't make sense. Now if they could only understand some Ayoré. . . .

An elderly man came up to Anna and began to feel her, running his fingers up and down her arms. Now what was that supposed to mean? Another man came and grabbed him, abruptly pulling him away. Shivers of fear overtook her momentarily as her now activated mind reminded her of the awful stories of those hostile people. A glance at John gave no relief. In the darkness it seemed his face was as white and drawn as hers.

Unexpectedly there was a lull in the hubbub. Now what? A bobbing flashlight beam was coming towards them. Then, just as suddenly the din crescendoed as the group members swarmed around the light. John and Anna caught glimpses of a white man. This must be a missionary!

Len Barrett, a single man in his early fifties and the only missionary at home just then had come to join his people in their welcome jaunt. Relaxing after a full day, Len had removed his hearing aid, and had failed to notice the commotion until now. His welcome was warm and hearty although there was hardly space to express it. The chatter and eagerness surrounding him and demanding his attention, spoke of the love and acceptance he had earned.

"The brother wishes to apologize to the white lady. He says Sueriadé touched her. He did it because he is blind but still had a desire to *see* her. However, they all feel badly about this display of bad manners."

Len's explanation warmed Anna's heart, and his further comments shed more light on their questions. The reason behind their royal reception was the four o'clock radio message received by the missionary, announcing John and

Anna's planned arrival time. Upon hearing the first distant sounds of an approaching vehicle the enthusiastic natives had rushed out on the road to meet them.

In bed that night, trying vainly to quiet a rapidly beating heart, Anna whispered, "Isn't it great that these people have already been reached? They have advanced so far. If I think back to what they were like a few years ago, that surprise meeting on the road could have turned out very differently."

"Could it ever!" The squeeze of John's hand on hers told of more emotion than his words. Feeling deeply the togetherness they both needed, they bowed once more in heartfelt thanks. The God who had brought them safely through this day was certainly worth praising.

PUESTO PAZ, the Place of Peace, a comparatively new Indian village and missionary compound had opened two years ago. To some seventy-five wandering nomads this had been a first attempt at settling down.

"It looks interesting, doesn't it? And it sure seems to be working out," John commented, after spending a few hours leisurely evaluating the place.

John and Anna spent a month watching, listening, and learning. To Anna it seemed that the more eagerly she tried to hear the distinct sounds of the conversation around her, the more hopelessly jumbled they became. The tone was a monotonous run-on rumble; every word sounded about the same as the next.

Another problem bothering Anna was the smell. Never before had it occurred to her how obnoxious this might become. Even at night when she could see no one around, she could tell, through the ever open windows, whenever a native came within reach of her senses. On numerous occasions this made her so nauseated that she knew she must pray for a miracle. She couldn't stand this any longer. The rather tart saying, "Follow your nose," coined by a fellow worker, was all too relevant. It served the purpose not only when looking for mission items, like the smoked ham Anna's brother had sent up from Paraguay, but also when trying to locate a neighbor.

Quite earnestly Anna began to pray about her problem. She knew that God would answer.

After this seemingly generous dose of getting the feel of a new language and culture they transferred back to Cochabamba for a six-week intensive language study of Ayoré. This meant eight hours of formal studies every day, plus two more of homework. By the end of this period they were expected to write their own testimony in that language, correctly and without help.

About halfway through their studies Anna suddenly became very ill. The doctor provided no relief and soon John rushed a very sick Anna to the hospital. This doctor diagnosed an acute kidney infection, and prepared to give her penicillin.

"Don't! Please don't!" Anna protested urgently. "I'm allergic to it. *Very allergic!"*

Perhaps she hadn't spoken clearly or correctly enough. Or perhaps he just wasn't inclined to listen. At any rate, he totally ignored her request. Very shortly he realized his mistake, but it was too late. Efforts to counter-attack the poison became frenzied and hectic. Anyone seeing her puffy face and hearing her labored, rasping breath sensed that it was a life or death matter. Eventually the battle was won; Anna was safely through one emergency. Was she ready to face another?

At first the strangely disorganized state of affairs at the hospital had seemed offensive, but Anna began to trust the team of doctors who worked with her. When they announced the need for surgery it felt like a bolt out of the blue, but their reasoning made sense. The unforseen surgery turned out to be major, an extensive repair job in the bladder area. Anna struggled for days in a very low state. The need for surgery had accumulated unnoticed as an after-effect of her hysterectomy in Manitoba several years before. It had mushroomed out of proportion and, unattended, would likely have killed her.

The third day was past and the crisis was over. Or so they thought. Suddenly her fever began to rise and it became evident that she was coming down with an attack of malaria. Her former doctor's prophecy that malaria would be a thing of the past had not come true after all. When the mercury in the thermometer climbed to the top there was another time of hustling, of alarm in the air. In unique Spanish terms the doctor cursed the day. No one really blamed him. To have three separate dire emergencies on one patient within a few days was a lot to take.

"Without God's special grace, I wouldn't do any better," John thought.

Slowly but surely the medication took effect and after twenty-four hours that crisis too was over. For the first time now John dared stay home to study. For the first time, Anna noticed, she was getting some quiet time. The nurses and doctors were not constantly hovering over her. The time had come—she could have her *think!*

Sorting out her thoughts did not come easy. "Why, God, why?" was the question that kept coming, as if to torment her, no matter how gallantly she pushed it aside. Why would God do all this to her when she was giving her all to Him? She soon realized what she must do. That question must be remodelled. Instead of the *why* of self-pity and frustration, she must ask, "What good are you sending through this, Lord? What am I to learn from this?" Even then the question had no immediate answer.

After a week's stay at the hospital she was released to the mission home. Her condition, however, necessitated a lengthy recuperation period as well as constant proximity to the doctor's care. At the end of the six-week course, John reluctantly prepared to leave for Puesto Paz without her.

"I hate to do this, Anna. I . . . er . . . I certainly didn't plan it this way."

"I know, Dear. I'll be okay. Very soon I'll follow you —

you'll be surprised." She had to be optimistic. She had to be brave, she told herself. Why let on that she was actually both scared and worried?

One specially warm kiss and hug and he was gone. Alone now, Anna had to face the long quiet hours of convalescence.

The next several weeks became oppressive. Anna began to wrestle anew with the ever present question of "Why?" She struggled to cope and overcome the devastating waves of homesickness for John and the children. If only she could have one glimpse of even one of her loved ones. There was no way — not even a phone call to shorten the miles or stop the bleeding of her heart.

"Oh, God," she cried in desperation. She knew herself only too well. It would be so natural, so easy to press the panic button and yield to despair. Couldn't God have thought of an easier way for her to serve him?

"God," her plea held all the depth of longing within her. *"I want to grow. I want to grow up in You and be strong. But I'm so weak, so hopelessly weak. . . ."*

A sob escaped her frail and tired body. Then another and another. Finally the floodgates opened and she cried unabashedly.

Should she simply yield to the awful temptation and give up? No, she would pray again. She must keep praying.

"Lord, God, You have taught me so much in the past. Help me to remember. Help me to apply now what I've learned . . . And please, *please,* show me at least some of Your reasons, some of Your purpose behind all this."

As her heart became quiet before God, an expectant hush came over her. Then, like a whispering of the leaves in a gentle breeze, ever so kindly but with the sound of authority, the answers began coming. God's old-time promise of "I will never leave thee nor forsake thee" (Hebrew 13:5) was true after all, and a feeling of appreciation filled her as she began to see where the pieces of the puzzle fit.

"'My thoughts are not your thoughts, neither are your

ways My ways . . . For as the heavens are higher than the earth, so are my ways higher than your ways, and My thoughts than your thoughts' (Isaiah 55:8,9). You thought you could not bear the separation from your children. I knew I could supply you with strength to bear even greater separations than that; yes, also from your husband, and in the midst of strangers. Later you will understand better what I had in mind. For now you must simply learn to lean hard on Me. You must learn to let go of everything and everybody and simply trust Me. *Yes, simply trust Me.* 'My strength is made perfect in weakness . . . My grace is sufficient for thee' (2 Cor. 12:9).

"My purpose is to fill you with Myself and all my fullness and power. I am able to do 'exceedingly abundantly above all that you ask or think' (Ephesians 3:20). That is the power I am promising you. Are you willing? Or do you want to plan your own life?"

"No, God. I am willing. Make me more willing. I want Your way in my life."

The heat and pressure of the struggle were gone. Instead, Anna had peace. Those verses from God's Word were so old and familiar but today they seemed new and real and relevant. She must remember never to take them for granted again. She would get up and mark them in her Bible. She would hide them forever in her heart.

THE MISSION Aviation plane was ready to take off. Anna was in it and so were her children who had just been picked up from school. Her convalescence was over and her heart was light. The feeling reminded her of a gruelling exam time followed by relief and joy when the teacher announces, "You made it!"

The plane settled into its course across the jungle. Every now and then the constant greenery below was spotted with a rocky peak or crisscrossed with winding ribbons of river. Somewhere down there were the people God had called them to minister to, but today that thought could not take priority. She sensed that God understood. Today, after four months of sepration from her children, she was together with them. They had laughed and cried and hugged and chattered. Yes, they were together now. Together they were going home, home to Daddy, home to John. Soon they would see it — Puesto Paz! Very soon, oh, it would be good just to fall into her husband's arms. The six weeks without him had seemed awfully long.

In a few days it would be Christmas. Just think of it. Christmas! Their first Christmas here. Suddenly it didn't matter that they would not have a house of their own. It didn't matter that no one had baked and shopped and decorated and prepared for Christmas in a normal way. No, it didn't matter. They had each other. That was important. And they had God. That was even more important.

Even before the plane had taxied to a full stop, they saw John. His warm, welcoming smile matched their eagerness, as each child scrambled for the quickest exit. John hugged Anna as the children gathered around. It was so good to be together. The large ring of undaunted enthusiastic admirers bothered Anna a little. It earned gasps and stares from the children, who were greatly excited about their first encounter with natives. However, warmth, love and togetherness surpassed all other feelings as they made their way to the house. Today God seemed only kind, good and gracious. It was a thrill just to be alive.

That night, vainly willing herself to sleep, Anna suddenly remembered something. She had noticed no smell although she had been close enough to the natives. She roused John and questioned him. How could the situation have changed so fast?

"It's not they who have changed. It's you," John laughed.

"Then God has answered my prayer. I'd almost forgotten about it," Anna mused. "I'm so glad."

The smell of the people never bothered her again.

THE CHRISTMAS holidays slipped by all too fast. Again the children were gone. It was time for Anna to join the working force. At first this meant the same thing for Anna as it did for her husband. Mornings were spent in the books, learning and ever learning more, in their all-out effort to master the language. The afternoons were taken up with fellowship amongst the neighbors. They would sit with them, walk with them and talk with them, or at least try. John, ahead in learning the language, would lead the way. Together they worked at making friends and ever trying to communicate.

The day came that Anna was to try out a working responsibility. John had for some time been actively involved in community set-up, agricultural planning and physical work related to that. Anna's choice was between literacy class or the medical work. Since the only other lady missionary was already managing the medical work, Anna decided to be agreeable and try the teaching position.

Almost from the start, she felt she was in the wrong place. After her doubts had been building for days, she confided in John. "I think I've made the wrong decision. I don't feel God's peace and blessing on my job. I tell myself to like it and sometimes I sort of do, but I always feel it's a put-on. I keep feeling it's not what God planned for me."

"Let's pray about it then," John encouraged. "God will show us what to do."

Anna agreed. Yet the two sides to her situation stubbornly and persistently kept churning in her mind. There was her heart's desire that she'd had almost as long as she could remember, to be involved in medical work. None of her co-workers knew this, however. Should she tell? The question made her feel shy and unworthy, especially since her co-worker was already doing the job, and appeared efficient and happy enough at it. Anna had no desire to be querulous or selfish. Finally she prayed, like John suggested, and committed the problem to the Lord. He would solve it.

After several days of waiting and praying, John announced

his intention. "I'm ready to do something. Let's broach the subject at our coming staff meeting and see what happens." Happily Anna agreed.

They were amazed at how smoothly God worked it out. Although the proposal was at first greeted with surprise, very soon the rest of the staff received the same conviction John had. God wanted Anna in the medical work.

Walking home after the meeting, Anna recalled an old Bible verse she used to know and love. How did it go again? Didn't it promise something about getting the desires of your heart? She must look it up.

There it was. Psalm 37: 4 and 5. "Delight thyself also in the Lord and He shall give thee *the desires of thy heart.* Commit thy way unto the Lord; trust also in Him and He shall bring it to pass."

Although this work gave her satisfaction and joy from the very beginning, outwardly it provided innumerable frustrations. Because she was still slow with the language she felt clumsy, although she soon found that the pressing daily needs helped her learn faster. Every day she picked up a new phrase or two.

The extreme need of medical work greatly shocked and almost overwhelmed her. If she had not been directly involved. Anna would never have believed the heavy work load.

The child delivery needed her immediate attention. The natives worshipped the bird god, a little night owl which could put terrible curses on anyone. Steeped as they were in superstition, they believed that newborn babies were especially susceptible to such a curse. Any problem during the delivery, a long, hard case, twins, a breech baby or "feet-first" delivery or any abnormality, even as minor as a missing toe, was reason enough for the baby to be buried alive at once. The more promptly this was done, the more effectively the god would be appeased. The same curse fell on any baby born out of wedlock or of a father who had deserted the mother. There was no chance to reconsider nor any allowance for mourning.

A good Ayoré woman would never moan or cry, no matter how difficult the delivery. Traditionally, as a nomadic people, the place to deliver was a secret spot somewhere behind a tree or a thick underbush. *No one,* not even the husband, could know of her case until it was all over. Then and only then could she appear back in the village and present, hopefully, a healthy child. If the baby didn't make the grade, a spot of loosened earth was the only evidence of what had happened, and the haunted look on the mother's face the only proof of her sorrow. Maybe next year the bird god would give her another chance. Just maybe he'd deal more kindly and there wouldn't be the curse.

For more than two years now missionaries had been working hard, teaching patiently, bit by bit. Change never came dramatically. On one hand the people were hopelessly entangled in their traditional taboos and fears. On the other there was evidence of deep hunger and longing for a better way. The Jesus way that the workers had taught them seemed to be the answer. And yet, did they really want it? Could they let go of tradition, get rid of the curse, and experience peace instead?

When Anna accepted the medical responsibility, the natives were already living in houses which the missionaries had taught them to make. Crude places with earthen floors, but a great improvement from the wild jungle. And the people had learned to sleep on beds made with poles.

The traditional delivery custom was not throbbing with change. However, the situation was delicate and Anna knew she was treading on thin ice. Any false move on her part could cause a serious flare-up and really disrupt the peace. She found comfort in knowing there was a senior missionary around for advice. She relied heavily on the promises that were by now clearly marked in her well-worn Bible.

Because the deliveries now took place in their houses, the fathers would summon the missionary nurse for help. This

106

had ended the original secrecy. After a lot of persuasion the missionaries had convinced the people to abandon the practice of baby killings. Finally it had made sense. God loved each one of them, not only the fittest. But give up all their taboos? That was unthinkable. If God loved all people, that was fine. But surely the bird god was also still actively around and it only made sense that he would now center his curse on something else. They decided it was the placenta and so it became their new law that this must be buried very promptly under the bed. Nobody must touch it, not even the nurse. If anyone should, by mistake, the curse he'd receive would surely be most dreadful.

Anna was called to her first delivery while the other missionary was away. With butterflies busy in her stomach and a strange mixed feeling of utter helplessness and yet complete dependence on God, she set out. Her flashlight beaming bravely ahead, showing the path, she suddenly felt like singing.

"My God and I walk through this vale together,
We walk and talk as good friends should and do. . . ."

The delivery went well and each one thereafter became a little easier as Anna gained confidence. The words of that song cheered her as she struggled to counteract dejection in her daily work with the children's health problems. The fact that most of these seemed to be caused by dirt, ignorance and malnutrition didn't make the job any easier.

"If only I could wipe out their negligence," she chastised herself, "I could wipe out a large percentage of their illness." And yet, wasn't that the very challenge of her work here?

One night she decided to pen the lines that kept entering her mind. The poem was later published in the missions's field paper.

Compassion
I shivered with disappointment
as the small grimy hand

slid hesitantly into my own.
I looked with disgust at the dirty
tangled hair full of scabies,
and wondered when that filthy face
and the dirty clothes had last been washed.
I saw the runny nose
and bare feet on the cold morning grass.
Yes, it added up to
one of those countless infections
that could only be cured by injections.
I saw brown, frightened, pleading eyes
force tears down her dirty cheeks
as they caught sight of the needle.
My heart cried out for her
and for her mother who doesn't know
the value of a child being clean.
So many times the mother'd been told
the value of cleanliness,
but she still doesn't understand.
And then I felt Jesus reach out through me
to help and love that filthy brown face,
with compassion that He alone can give.
Then I wondered how many more
brown frightened faces there are
that would look up to someone
if they only had a chance.
What about you? Wouldn't you like to feel
Jesus reaching out through you
to help brown, pleading faces?

Chapter Ten

THE PLACE was in chaos.

A measles epidemic, a dreaded thing in any tribal camp, had broken out. A group of some thirty wandering nomads had arrived from Paraguay shortly before. Apparently they brought the bug with them, for the original Puesto Paz residents that were old enough had all been immunized.

It was about a week before their second Christmas on the field when Anna diagnosed the first case. In an effort to prevent spreading, she isolated the man in her own house. Soon she realized this was useless — his whole family had come down with the measles. Within a few days she found herself surrounded by twenty-six seriously ill patients, each flat in bed or on a mat on the ground.

To make the rounds and minister to each was more than a full load, but this was not nearly the end of it. Although Anna and John were still in part-time language study, she now had to drop these studies. Besides the usual work, they were beginning to build a house, a first-time experience here. To top it off Christmas was fast approaching. Anna had scarcely begun her plans and preparations. Any day now the children would be home. What joy that would add! Anna had yearned to make this Christmas a special joy, and a time of excitement for the children. Surely Christmas frills and thrills were made for children.

But now was no time to think about Christmas frills! The village babies that had not been immunized came down with measles too. Nine-month-old Anita, an especially lovable one, was one of the first. Named after Anna, chosen as godmother, and having been one of Anna's first deliveries, Anita filled a warm spot in Anna's heart. "My cute little black-eyed darling," she fondly called her. It stabbed her heart when the mother, a devout Christian, anxiously brought the baby to her for a check up. The youngster had acute measles combined with pneumonia.

Without further thought Anna took the baby into her hut for 'hospitalization.' She encouraged the mother to stay as well. This was done as a precaution to avoid suspicions and misunderstandings in case of further complications. She knew from the start it was going to be a stiff battle, but Anna threw herself into the fray as if the child were her own.

For forty-eight hours the struggle raged. There was no thought of sleep or rest! Whenever the baby seemed a little better, Anna would make the rounds among the twenty-six other patients. Medication, needles, loving care, or a gentle washing of burning foreheads — everyone needed something. Everyone wanted Anna! Anna kept moving from one to the next.

Then it was back into the room with little Anita. No effort was spared. Every known technique, every medication was faithfully administered with loving care. Just two days before Christmas! Anna noticed that the baby was failing, losing out. Would all their earnest prayers remain unanswered? Would all her hard work be for naught?

This was no time to reason things through. No time for thought. If she tried her head began to spin; her eyes began to ache. Blindly, determinedly, she continued working. If ever she was needed, it was now.

The children arrived! Numbly she greeted them during those hectic hours. She, who'd been so eager to see them; she who had planned a peaceful, exciting family Christmas! She hardly noticed her children. Where were the dreams for a happy Christmas? She couldn't remember. Did it matter?

Anna turned back to the baby. She picked it up and held it carefully, vainly attempting to ease the pain-racked breathing. Each breath was coming more slowly, with greater difficulty. The baby's color was changing to a deathly hue. Struggling to keep back her tears Anna realized the inevitable.

Suddenly the struggle was over. Anita had breathed her last breath while in Anna's arms. Surely her next would be in Jesus' arms, perhaps even now. Just as suddenly Anna became aware that the house was full of people. Everyone was squeezing in. The weeping and wailing that soon began was most awful to hear. The children watched with big eyes. Terror and awe was written all over their faces. What did all this mean? With questioning looks they clung to Mother or hovered at her heels.

"They are really getting initiated today," Anna murmured to herself, but there was no sharp edge left in her feelings. Right now, her own family came second.

Anna longed to help these dear people and erase their terrible sorrow. She knew there was no need for the wailing — Anita was safe with Jesus. But there seemed no way to communicate; no way to make them understand. Their minds were still too soaked in darkness.

Someone grabbed Anna's arm. "If you want to save the blanket and pillows the baby used, you had better do it quickly! If you don't someone will come and bury everything the baby touched, along with all her possessions."

Anna scooped up the blankets at once and tucked them safely behind a tree on the edge of the yard. She couldn't afford to lose her best blankets!

To declare someone dead was a new experience for Anna. The fact that it was her lovely Anita made this even more memorable and painful. Yet there seemed no time nor space to feel or think.

"Peace at last," Anna thought as she sought the comfort of her bed. "I could just drop, I'm so exhausted."

"Ah-h-h-h . . . !" a wild indescribable shriek pierced her thoughts.

"What was that?" she stammered as she hurried out to investigate. Her children, transfixed by the scene, stood and stared, unable to comprehend the situation.

Tamie, a handsome young man of the village and an uncle

to little Anita, had thrown himself into an open campfire. This was the best, the most fervent expression of sympathy for his bereaved sister. But those screams did not come from him — no, his mouth was firmly closed as he suppressed the agony. Instead, it was the onlookers who were going wild.

The smell of roasting flesh wafted to Anna. She shuddered! Those burns must be terribly deep. Another shudder of revulsion passed through her. What an awful sight. She certainly hadn't needed a new critical case on her emergency list. "I certainly don't need more work," she moaned as she questioned, "Oh, God, why do these natives learn so slowly? Are the missionaries at fault? Are they not teaching correctly, efficiently or thoroughly enough?"

Tamie's burns were deep, and Anna knew that the road to recovery would be a long, slow one. His right arm seemed almost beyond repair. Not once, however, did he express regret about his 'heroic' deed. Nor did he ever complain or moan about the pain. He had been true to his culture. He had been faithful. *IF YOU WANT TO SHOW LOVE AND SYMPATHY YOU MUST MAKE YOURSELF SUFFER.* There was no better way.

Even though this was the Christmas season, the epidemic afforded Anna few moments of rest. Towards the end of one of those busy Christmas days the family managed to gather around John and Anna. It was hard to find a quiet spot or a quiet hour. Whenever the family could get together for a few moments, each member guarded these precious moments. No one wanted any intrusions.

"It's strange," began Rachel, thoughtfully. "When we're at Tambo, it's almost like America. Now while we've been here with you, we've really seen something else. It's so different, I can hardly believe it."

"Yeah," interjected Albert. "I never would have believed it. I never knew that *anyone anywhere* suffered so helplessly and. . . ."

"And needed missionaries so desperately," finished

Arthur.

John was moved by the new insight the children revealed. He had a strong intuition that because of this Christmas they might never be the same again.

That night he spent extra time in prayer. "Oh, God, keep them. Keep them like this, close to You." The thought came again and again.

The changes were not very obvious to John or Anna at the time, but little by little they were revealed. Each of the children had gained new respect, not only for Mom and Dad, but for the whole field of missions. Their prayers became deeper intercession. They remembered to pray faithfully for Mom's long list of patients.

Finally, finally, after weeks of urgent, often desperate needs all about her, Anna's lull came. The epidemic was over, or so they thought. Most of the patients were now up and around; even the last slow cases were improving. Anna could occasionally find a few quiet minutes to commune with God. For a while these had been practically nil. The needs were so very urgent. And, when a crisis was over, Anna collapsed with exhaustion.

Anna had taken little time to read her Bible during these days. One thought that frequently interrupted her came from the Psalms: "Except the Lord build the house, they labor in vain that build it," and it seemed to be pointing its finger at her. Wasn't she laboring for the Lord? Surely it wouldn't be in vain!

Another nagging thought came from the book of James. So often Anna wanted to plan ahead, to count on the things that would happen tomorrow and then tomorrow. The camping style of life combined with the direct leadings of the Lord had been so unpredictable that the warning words of James were being hammered harshly into her system. "Go to now, ye that say, Today or tomorrow we will go into such a city, and continue there . . . Whereas ye know not what shall be on the morrow? For what is your life? It is even a vapor, that appeareth for a little while, and then vanishes away . . . Ye ought to say, *If the Lord will,* we shall live and do this or that." This was not new to Anna. This reminder had often come before but never had it been so forcefully relevant. Anna knew that she had learned a lot about living happily one day at a time, but this — this was too much! She caught herself rebelling at the 'moment by moment' idea. How fantastic it would be to have a structured life in which one could plan ahead. If only — but no, she must give this to God as well. Would she never be able to soar, to gain new heights, to graduate in this area?

Another group of wanderers appeared from somewhere in the jungle to join the village. This was one of those unpredictable 'norms' of their lifestyle, and one which God seemed determined to have them accept and perhaps even learn to like. The question Anna constantly faced was, could they do it?

Suddenly, the measles epidemic broke out in new proportions. What happened? Wasn't everyone immunized? Those newcomers! Apparently the germs had still been rampant on the grounds and the newcomers, without immunizations, had no resistance. Once more the yard was full of mats holding many very sick patients. Native culture demanded that sick persons lie as close to the ground as possible so that the sickness would return to the earth.

March came. The house that John was building was nearing completion. Slowly but surely the job had moved ahead. Now additional workers were needed. Two Bolivians were hired to plaster the walls and cement the floor. No matter how many other chores screamed for Anna's attention, she still needed to cook for the workers.

Anna sighed wearily as she put away the breakfast dishes. The nights were never long enough anymore; the pressure of a new day seemed just a little more than she could take. And yet . . . no, she must not sigh, she must not think of being tired. If she would just keep on, possibly hurry a little more, she would soon be finished with her morning duties. She must psyche herself up — think positively!

"Let's see now. Today is Thursday. Tomorrow the school children will be home. I better hurry. Hopefully there won't be too many emergencies or new patients on the sick roll. Then I can prepare for the children. This time everything must be nice for them. *Everything will be nice!*" she insisted to herself. "How pleased they'll be to see the new house almost ready."

The sigh was forgotten. With new zest and determination Anna turned to her work. Before she knew it she was humming a favorite tune. Her heart was light as she went to the medicine closet and proceeded to arm herself with the various supplies needed for her nursing round. Was this not the job that had given her complete fulfillment and deep joy? "Lord, you've been good to me," she whispered. Surely He would understand that she didn't have time to pray. The people out there were waiting.

Both of her hands were full — full of medications and needles for all the necessary injections. She hurried out. Eager faces were already pressed hard against the window screens. She had not noticed that the scatter rug on the cement floor had chosen to curl or get rumpled that morning. With hurried step she hastened out. Oops! Down she went, right on her back with a nasty thud! Supplies went flying, except for one syringe that stayed in Anna's outstretched hand. Anna did not move. She lay exactly where she'd fallen. "This is very strange," she thought. "I should get up." But there was nothing in her to put the thought into action. "I ought at least to make some effort and try," she declared to herself but her body simply refused to function. Not one iota of action could she force out of herself. "This is weird! I'm becoming a statute." Was she going into shock? She couldn't tell. Suddenly her world turned hazy and reality slipped . . . away. . . .

After the first gasps of surprise and a moment or two to gather their bearings, the faces at the window changed to people of wit and action. Someone urged native children to run

115

for John, busy at the site of the new airstrip. "Come quick," they screamed. "Come quick, Don Juan, Señora Anna has fallen and she cannot move. She cannot move one bit."

In the meantime several women began to work with Anna. Completely numb and paralyzed, Anna was unable to protest, even after she began to feel some pain. Systmatically, albeit very rougly, they massaged her all over, from neck to toe. As her feeling returned the pain became excruciating, but with it came life. By the time help arrived, she was moving around a bit.

"Wow! What happened?" John gasped out of breath from the quick run to find out what the children were screaming about. He was anxious to solve whatever needed solving for the sight before him gave him a stab of fear.

"I . . . why . . . I . . . help me up, John. I think I can get up now."

He and his co-worker lifted her slowly, gently, for in spite of her gallant effort to ignore the pain, her face was ashy gray. They could not help but notice her wince with each movement, and bite her teeth to suppress each moan.

"Let's see now." John investigated her lower back where she was having the terrible pain, and found swelling and ugly bruises. Neither he nor the other worker could find evidence of further injury.

"If that's the case," Anna said with typical grit and determination, "then I can hack this. I . . . I'll go back to work. It was stupid of me to fall in the first place."

It was hard, much harder than she had anticipated. Time and again tears streamed unheeded down her face as she suppressed the groans that wanted to come. Bending over the sick ones on their mats turned out to be, not only an agony in her back, but impossible. The only way was to fall down on her knees beside the patient and then grab someone's hand to help her back up. Yet, when she looked at the patients and saw the tears on their faces from their pain, when she saw how very sick some of them were, she knew she could not

116

quit. Pain or no pain, she must go on.

As scheduled, the children came home on Friday. Anna's beautiful plans to have things just so had not materialized. In spite of the family's plea for her to take a rest and give up the work for a little while, Anna kept on. Bravely, yes stubbornly, she worked. Several of the patients were really very critically ill, and in the absence of the other missionary couple, her work was indispensable. "I can't just leave them out there to die," she argued.

The pain was becoming more unbearable. It made her nauseated. Surely God would supply the needed grace. She hadn't thought to ask His advice, but hadn't Paul gone through countless sufferings and bravely, even cheerfully, borne them out? Wasn't it only right for her to do the same?

She plodded her way through Saturday, and even through Sunday. John and the children did everything they could to help and took over much of her work. However, nothing they did could prevent Anna from making regular rounds among the patients. Nor could anything be done to ease her pain. Because of her multiple allergies, taking pain killers was out of the question.

Early Monday morning, after a restless, sleepless night, her tune suddenly changed. Yes, after almost four days of agonizing pain and pushing herself to the limit, she had gotten more than weary. She had reached the end of her endurance. Whether it was hysteria or semi-delirium, John couldn't tell. All he knew was that Anna was not herself. In a voice that sounded odd and crackling, she fairly spat the words out. "I don't care. Let them all die. Everyone. I can't move another inch to help them. You'll have to get me out of here to see a doctor."

John had been praying earnestly for her. Now he wondered — maybe he should have gone against her strong will and ordered help. He'd wanted to respect her wishes, and he had admired her guts! Now the thought began to haunt him — maybe, maybe she was hurt more than they'd thought.

117

He knelt in silent prayer. When he got up, ready for action, he felt the hand of God on his shoulder, caring, approving, sustaining. It was the touch he needed as he sent off a radio message to Santa Cruz. All of their stations on the network immediately picked up the news of Anna's accident. Before noon the plane arrived, took the children back to school, and dropped Anna off at Santa Cruz.

Fred Kalne, a missionary at Santa Cruz, picked her up and took her to the clinic for X-rays. The doctor scolded her soundly before telling her what he found. She should have come in much sooner. Her injury was serious. The pelvic bone was fractured, the tail bone broken completely two inches up from the end and a huge blood clot had formed in that badly bruised area. She would need to go to the hospital to have the bones set and be put into a cast. The cast, like a heavy corset, would be around her waist and hips, from the chest down but keeping her legs free to move and even walk.

"Wow, I should have known it was something serious," Anna admonished herself wearily.

The doctor, unfamiliar with her records, ignored her request for no anesthetic. Surely she needed at least some help to endure the agony of the bone setting. With horror he quickly realized she was right. Would he have a chance to tell her how he regretted his decision? Her body's extreme reaction to the mild anesthetic caused her heart to stop. Quickly a heart machine was attached. It saved her for the moment, as frantic efforts by the staff continued in attempts to save her life.

Three hours later, after eight injections of celestone, she finally awoke. She was in a different room, where Fred Kalne was watching her very gravely.

"What's going on?" she wondered, only half awake. Slowly she pieced the story together. She had been near death. Everyone had been frantically working on her. Because she wasn't expected to make it, someone called the mission house. Could anyone please come?

Efforts had been made to reach John. When they finally

got through the next morning, the mission plane was busy elsewhere. Rather than delay any longer, he decided to come by truck. When he got there she was over the worst. Together they thanked God for sparing her life.

The doctor had strong feelings about Anna's case. "I never want to touch you medically again," he blurted out, quite unceremoniously. "I have no desire to be responsible for the death of a missionary." She sensed that he was not unfeeling; he cared, and, that she'd better believe him for he meant what he said.

Because of the extremity of her allergy problems, a far-reaching decision was made. From now on she must carry with her at all times and under all situations, a clear warning identification or alert sign written in more than one language, so that anyone working with her would be sure to understand. And, once she got the bracelet, she was never again to be seen without it.

The actual setting of the bones and making of the cast was no small thing. Comparing it, however, with the earlier emergency it wasn't as bad as anticipated. Slowly, normalcy returned. John stayed for a few days but when he saw that Anna would be alright, the call of the work pulled him back.

"I hate to leave you, Anna," he ventured. Neither had forgotten how difficult the forced separation had been last year. The urgent need at home, however, tugged at him, doing battle with the all-too-fresh memories of the recent emergency for Anna. Which was more important?

"I'll be alright," Anna returned, trying gallantly to be strong and brave. His reluctance to go did much to take away the secret hurt. What she didn't say, however, was the nagging thought which kept sneaking into her mind. *"This really isn't fair!"* Never would she have admitted it, not even to herself, but a very subtle form of bitterness (or was it self-pity) appeared determined to engulf her. And it seemed there wasn't a thing she could do about it.

Anna's pain was comparatively minimal now, and since

she wasn't on any drugs, her mind soon found itself working overtime. It seemed the umpteenth time that she was flat on her back, convalescing from something or other. Why did God keep doing this to her? Or were the doings her own? Could it be Satan behind there somewhere, like in the story of old-time Job? . . . Why? . . . Why? . . .

Why was this happening? They had been on the field for almost two years. By now she was really into the medical work which she heartily enjoyed. Not only did she like the work, she thrived on the feeling of being so absolutely needed. And, she knew she'd made good; she was efficient, reliable and loved. How could God, if He was loving and just, take her out of there in the middle of a crisis? Perhaps even now the babies, the sickest ones, were dying. Anna's bed and cast became stifling, prison chains. With all her heart she longed to go back to work. She wanted to . . . she wanted. . . . "Oh God don't you know what I want? Aren't you there?"

As night is often darkest just before the sun breaks through, so went Anna's struggle that day. Suddenly her thoughts turned. Why, God had not asked her what she wanted! He had plans for her, plans that were different than her own. Suddenly, as that thought overcame her, she was filled with remorse. She remembered the promise made in this very hospital. Was it only last year? She had committed herself to wanting God's way, not her own. Not once had she noticed herself forgetting. She'd been too busy, too preoccupied with all the needs around her. Now, as though taking off a soiled garment and looking at the dirt in disgust, she saw herself; self-sufficient (it was so hard to admit this to herself), but also proud. It was incredible! Her own capital "I" had come to the forefront. "It is *my* work. *I* am needed. *I* am fulfilled here. *I* like it."

"Oh, no!" she turned in shame to the Lord, "I didn't want to become like that. Lord, help me! Show me how I can change."

She got out her Bible. As it fell open to Psalm sixty-three, she began reading. Some of the lines stood out boldly.

'"Oh, God, early will I seek thee; my soul thirsteth after thee, my flesh longeth for thee in a dry and thirsty land!' *When have I last longed for God with all my heart?*

'"To see thy power and thy glory . . .' *Why, I tried to show my own power and see my own glory, didn't I?*

'"My soul shall be satisfied as with marrow and fatness, my mouth shall praise thee with joyful lips when I remember thee upon my bed and meditate on thee in my night watches.' *Oh dear, I was always too busy or too tired to remember You very long, God, not even in the night watches. No wonder You couldn't give me the marrow and the fatness.*

'"My soul followeth hard after thee.' *I followed hard after the work, Your work, Lord, but I've forgotten to follow hard after You."*

Her 'why?' had found its answer. "Your work is just what I want it to be," a voice seemed to be saying. "You are doing well too, but your attitude must change, or you'll be headed for shipwreck. Your love and loyalty to me must come first, always first. Without that you will run yourself ragged; you will miss the best blessings and you simply cannot bring glory to My name."

She read the Psalm again and again, and again, until it was seared into her mind. Finally she could pray, "God, Lord Jesus, *You* shall be first. Help me to remember. You are always first, always more important than my work or anything else."

Then she remembered! Somewhere she had heard a preacher speak vehemently. One thought had stood out above all the others. "God loves you so much that He would gladly break your leg or knock you over the head with a two-by-four to attract your attention and draw you to Him!"

Was it true? How far fetched it had seemed then. Today it seemed more plausible. Hadn't God let her break her back to attract her attention? Maybe that was it! He had coveted her first love. She dabbed at a tear, a tear of joy, not self-pity.

The love of Jesus suddenly seemed so real and precious, Anna wanted to do nothing else than spread that love around wherever she went as long as she lived.

A few day later she was ready to go home. Although Anna was in a pensive mood, she soon responded to the friendly Missionary Aviation Fellowship (MAF) pilot who flew her home. They chatted congenially most of the way.

"It will be something else, walking around with this big cast!" Anna commented. "The cast is so heavy and clumsy." She wasn't used to it yet, and now she would need to walk amongst the natives. She was certain they would clamor all over her. "But I'm glad to be going back," she concluded cheerfully.

Very soon after landing she hobbled around among the patients. Two had died during her absence, an eight-year-old girl and a fifty-year-old mother. She need not feel guilty. Anna found she could just leave these things in the hand of the Lord. He was in charge. Such a change in her priorities made her feel like a new person.

At her three-week check-up the bone specialist told Anna that her tail bone had grown in crooked. She would need surgery. Because they found no inner assurance about this, John and Anna persuaded the doctor to leave it. It never bothered her again.

One of his comments, however, brought smiles a few times. "You'd better put some fat on first, if you ever plan to fall again."

"How about it?" John teased. "If we accept the true Bolivian culture, you had better! Why, when you are as skinny as you are now, you prove me to be a bad husband, a poor provider. Put on some fat and you prove my goodness to you."

"Maybe I'd better," she responded lightly. Some of her natural sparkle was back and her smile was warm. It was good, really good, just to be alive.

ANNA had stood at the window for some minutes now,

waiting for the sunrise. She observed the light cast weird shadows around her as it found its way through all the dense, thorny foliage, vines and wild pineapple. She loved this time of day. And, she needed it, for this was the time to get in touch with God, with John, with herself.

Today however she keenly felt loss; a vital part was missing. That vital link was John, who had needed to overnight in town, as part of a little business trip. Once she would get into the swing of the day's activities, she wouldn't mind as much, but mornings and evenings were always rough.

She poured herself a cup of coffee. Reflecting on things, she knew she was spoiled. Almost always it was John who got up first. He was the one who'd go to the kitchen to make some coffee or 'yerba' tea. He liked nothing better than to bring her a cup before she was fully dressed. Then they'd sit together for a few minutes to plan the day and chat a bit, often hand in hand. Sometimes they'd read Scripture together; many times they would end up kneeling together in prayer.

She wasn't inclined to hurry today as she sat there, just reminiscing. "I have so much to be thankful for," she told herself. "Our marriage must be above average . . . Oh, we've had our hassles, as I imagine everyone does, but we always bounce back. Every squabble we've had, we've made up rather quickly, which is so much more fun anyway."

A vision of them sitting together on the ground at the remains of a campfire — not an unusual sight after a noon meal — floated through her mind. She saw again how he deliberately lingered a few extra minutes just to share or exchange news. "A good relationship is worth working at and spending time on," he'd proclaim, "and healthy, open communication is about the best way to do it."

A friend had teasingly suggested it was time they go on a second honeymoon. "The second?" John had blurted out. "We are still on our first!"

Anna smiled at the thought. She must remember to thank him for that kind of leadership. The morning's lonely coffee

123

refreshed her memory. She dare not take such a thing for granted.

Chapter Eleven

ONE thought had lain heavily on John's mind for some time. On numerous occasions he had laid plans, but for some reason had always shelved them again. Now it was summer. The children were home and the oldest were well able to help. Surely this must be the time!

Scott White, the son of Dr. John White of Winnipeg, had arrived to spend his vacation. Since his parents had been missionaries at a similar place, he was really interested in discovering the deeper aspects of the missionary challenge. His Bible school studies during the winter had given him a further desire to see things firsthand.

"Yes," mused John," "The time has come. We must move out now."

After some earnest prayer, John, together with Len Barrett, confirmed that decision. *The time had come!* The unreached Ayoré must be contacted. They would form a search party, or survey party, to look for the unreached. Perhaps they could make a contact. Scott, as well as Albert and Arthur, was eager to join. Three Ayoré Christian men also joined the expedition.

The bustling activity was exciting in itself. The Ayoré became totally involved. The women helped Anna with the baking for the trip, possibly a two-week trip. The men would take food, water, gas and oil on the truck; drive as far as they could, and then walk into the jungle.

They were off — into no man's land! No people and no roads! The only trails were the 'brechas' made by oil companies. Like a huge checkerboard, these 'brechas' had been made by bulldozers which had cleared paths, crisscrossing all through the jungle.

For almost two weeks Anna and the rest of the family prayed and waited. So did the Ayoré. Would everyone return safely? Would they reach the unreached? The daily radio contacts helped a lot to drive away the apprehension. Finally the party returned! What a royal welcome! This welcome was, however, spattered so heavily with questions that the answers couldn't come fast enough.

Yes, they had seen evidence of a very recent hermitage . . .No, they had not seen any Ayoré . . . Yes, they had noticed numerous Ayoré shoe marks!

Gradually everyone calmed down enough for the leaders to outline their finds. They had found the following in three distinct places.

1) They found some trees cut down and cleared out for honey in the typical Ayoré manner.

2) They found turtle shells beside ashes from overnight fires. The shells were opened in the exact Ayoré manner. The ashes of the campfire indicated that this was a fairsized group.

3) Tracks crossed the 'brechas.' Ayoré shoe marks were the tell-tale giveaway. Traditional Ayoré shoes are made of thick heavy tapir hides, with holes pierced into a square at places. String made of cactus fibre keeps the shoes in place. Heavy knots at one end secure the string, which then goes between the toes and around the ankle before coming down to be tied securely with heavy knots in the other two holes.

4) John also brought home a gourd with some remains of honey in it. The bees were still busy finishing the last bit.

Ayoré make their containers out of gourds. They fill these with fresh honey, stick in a bunch of cactus fibre, and let that get saturated. The Ayoré suck the honey out of the fibre and enjoy a long-lasting treat.

When Anna saw the gourd and held it in her hands, she was deeply moved. "I am holding a gourd that was previously held by a totally unreached person." Her thoughts became a prayer. "Lord, please allow us to hold hands with these people, to find them in order to help them." She knew this was dangerous. The prayer could explode on her. But regardless of that possibility, she meant it with all her heart.

The group had encountered no one nor had they heard or seen any movements or immediate signs of human life. After John had shot a deer for meat, several had thought they heard a sound behind them in the jungle. When nothing came of it they weren't sure.

Almost overnight, the people in the village expressed a new attitude and vision. A new zeal inspired them, and unexpressed desires were expressed. Suddenly each Christian remembered someone — a loved one still out there in the jungle: a brother, a sister, an aunt, a cousin. A great question hung over the group. "When can we go again and really find them?"

Three weeks later the answer came very unexpectedly. John received an emergency radio message from employees of the Western Oil Company (a U.S. enterprise). It seemed, one of their Bolivian employees had been killed — coldly murdered. While another man was operating a bulldozer, this man had been on foot, driving in the marker posts. The killer, who they suspected was an Ayoré Indian, had apparently come up from behind and taken him completely unawares. When the bulldozer operator found the body of his friend, he was almost paralyzed with fright. Would *he* make it out of this place alive?

In Ayoré culture the typical way to attack is to shoot at your target from the front, aiming for his middle. When the victim bends over in pain, trying perhaps to remove the twelve-inch arrow, the assailant comes from behind to finish the job by stabbing through the back with a lance and then tying him to the ground with a cord. In this way they expect to keep the victim's spirit in the ground at that spot and hopefully prevent it from following the killer. The weapons are left with the victim, but may be reclaimed after a year if the spirits haven't taken them.

Their reason for killing is often like choosing the lesser of two evils. The option of not killing in any sticky situation means that they are likely to make other mistakes instead, which in turn will invoke the curse of the gods and put them into a much worse situation than a *mere* killing would. Then too, killing is considered a sport, the BIG CHALLENGE OF MANHOOD.

John rushed to the railroad station to check out the story. Some of the oil workers were there to give further details.

John and Paul hurried home to prepare for the expedition. At a meeting at home they carefully explained, "We need volunteers to go with us, but we can take only those who will go for the Lord. There must be absolutely no fighting or killing. Each one who goes must be willing to give his life for the sake of the gospel."

An awesome hush hovered over the meeting momentarily, before eight decided. They did not hesitate long. Their willingness to give themselves was a touching sight. Their excited wives stood firmly with them. Very soon questions arose, "Whom will they find? My relatives?" Within a day John, Paul and the eight Ayoré were ready to go. They left Friday afternoon. John kept a diary and his own words tell the story best.

Saturday, September 10

"We arrived at the Oil Company base about 150 kilometers east of Puesto Paz. We checked the weapons found with the victim to make sure they were Ayoré. They were. The government had already sent out twelve soldiers to protect the Oil Company personnel. These men — workers and soldiers — were already in the process of moving out all equipment. The company was ready to quit and move out for good.

"The day before the killing, the group had been attacked, but was able to hide in the iron 'box car' in which it was travelling. Many arrows had whizzed by over the heads of the workers, but no one was injured.

"Now the military wanted to go with Paul and me to protect us. We had a difficult time persuading them not to. The Ayoré were already bitter from old war memories, and now freshly aroused, no doubt, by the latest events, would be terribly upset. Even ordinarily they tended to equate green uniforms with evil men for whom death was the mildest possible punishment.

"When I told them that we were also soldiers, soldiers of the cross, fighting in obedience to our King, they were frankly puzzled, but I thought I saw a new little gleam of respect.

"We finally decided that they would go with us to the site of the last attack, where they had pulled out the swamp buggy, and then return.

"This is what we did. When they were gone, the ten of us huddled together for special prayer. After that we were ready for action. Paul and I, with one Ayoré to stick up for us in case of need, stayed with the trucks at this site, to watch and pray, and to prepare food for the gang.

"The other seven Ayoré men set off in search of the savage ones. Right beside us they began to find clues. They picked up a well camouflaged trail, one that I would never have spotted. They could tell which direction had been travelled. By four o'clock they found the group's campsite which had been abandoned about a day or two before. Darkness overtook them and they spent the night."

Sunday September 11

"Around nine in the morning the men returned to eat and share. They had discovered and salvaged items the group had thrown out in their haste to get away. Obviously the group was fleeing. Our men set out shortly to follow and hopefully catch up.

"At 4:00 p.m. they did just that. They'd been following closely for awhile. The fact that the group had divided into two had not sufficed to divert the pursuers as the fleers had hoped.

"Ehoadide, the leader of our men, led the way. The savages turned now and greeted them with blood-curdling screams. Joboi, their leader, as well as the recent killer of the Bolivian oil worker, advanced with his lance drawn.

"Ehoadide spoke up. 'I not bad, I am *good* Ayoré, I not kill or fight.'

"Joboi screamed, 'Come closer, I will stab you.'

"Ehoadide continued calmly, ' I have come to help you. I am a good Ayoré.'

"The threat was repeated vehemently. 'Come closer. I want to kill you.'

"Neither of them made a move. Then Ehoadide threw away his weapon and lifted up his empty hands. 'See,' he said, 'I am not afraid. I will not fight. I am your friend.'

"Suddenly there was a stirring in the group. The old chief was speaking, trying to get their attention. 'Stop,' he called out with authority. *'Listen.* That man is speaking our language.' Apparently they hadn't noticed until then.

"Upon the old man's request the weapons were dropped and a semblance of peace gained. Our men explained about the trucks and us white men. Their group had reunited and counted a total of twenty-seven. Till very recently they had numbered more than twice that, but many had died through measles.

"Paul and I were just talking with our wives by radio contact when suddenly we saw them coming, the whole bunch of them. We must have frightened the girls some. We just blurted the news into the radio. It seemed our men had persuaded them, without too much problem, to come this far. Now the next tasks were before us.

"When they saw me at the truck, one woman came up to me and exclaimed, 'Boy, you are tall!' Several people joined her, and I got the impression they thought they knew me. I couldn't figure it out, until one fellow asked, 'Where are your other white men? There were five, when we saw you a moon ago.'

"I was puzzled. *It couldn't be,* and yet upon questioning, I found that it was. It seemed incredible. When the five of us, and the three Ayoré had been on that survey trip, we had come within several hundred yards of their camp. Very closely they'd watched our every move. They had followed us around.

"After I had shot that deer, there had been noise amongst them. Their cries of alarm were the sound we thought we'd heard. When I had taken a long walk alone — against our own rules — I had been followed closely. They said the fact that I carried a gun had saved my life. Their tone of voice convinced me that their respect for our weapons was akin to reverence.

"Suddenly they began to question us. Why had we been there? What did we want? Why weren't we scared? Why did we come back? What was the meaning behind all this?

"Together with the help of the others I tried to explain. We wanted to find them so we could help them. We wanted to be their friends. We loved them.

"When these truths began to register, their response was overwhelming. I couldn't believe it. Probably for the first time in my life I sympathized with Paul, of many years back, for his problem when the people wanted to crown him as a god. Eagerly now the people swarmed around me, exclaiming, 'You are brave. You are good. We will follow you. You will be our chief.' To stop them was impossible. Before I really noticed what was happening, they had the chief's crown and proceeded to crown me. They got out a collar of beautiful feathers and put it on me. Proudly, happily, they pronounced me their new 'chief.'

"What should I do? To convince them of their error was impossible under the conditions; to resist forcibly was unthinkable. So I submitted. In the future there'd be safer times to teach them things, I hoped."

Ayoré culture demands that a crown be worn by the chief (and chief only) at his coronation, as well as when going to battle. They also hold that every tiger is actually a retired or dead chief, and every would-be chief must successfully kill a tiger before he can be crowned. (Because of John's unusual bravery in their eyes, he could be exempted from this rule.) The crown is made of a strip of tiger skin and is decorated in the back with pretty bird feathers from their bird god. A long string of beads is slung across the chest in a certain special way. A fancy collar of feathers from many different birds, all descendants of the bird god, is then put on. This collar is the symbol of power in war. All of these must be worn together by the chief on these occasions, although he remains otherwise in the nude.

"When the air was clear enough for face-to-face discussion, Ehoadide asked the leader, 'Why did you think we were not Ayoré?'

" 'Because you look different. You have short hair,' was the ready reply. No doubt the fact that our people wore clothes had something to do with it too.

" 'And why did you not kill me when you said you would?'

"Again the answer was clear. 'Each time I wanted to, my arm stiffened. I could not move it to kill you.'

" 'Praise God,' I whispered under my breath.

"During the first available moments, Paul and I had radioed our wives again, asking them to contact Western Oil Company. The women were to update them on the latest development and ask for trucks to come help us take the new people to Puesto Paz.

"By radio contact the military commander asked, 'Can I come along?' My answer was 'Only if you take off your uniform.' He did. Together with the company representative and a Bolivian driver, they'd be on their way bringing one big truck. They should arrive the following morning.

"In the meantime we were *stuck* with the group of savage people. Sleep was out of the question. Every so often a spirit of restlessness could be felt. Shifty glances from the wild piercing eyes were enough to send goose bumps up anybody's spine. Poisoned arrows and lances remained constantly with them, ready for any spur-of-the-moment need.

"Ayoré are avid storytellers and our men soon showed this talent — a talent I now learned to appreciate with all my heart. They had gotten a vision of what they could do to keep peace. By morning they had in very picturesque language and in their own unique versions, told every Bible story they knew, as well as given a detailed description of the mission with its various functions and purpose. Only one attempt to escape was made. The runaway lady was soon caught by two men, one of ours and one of her own."

Monday, September 12

"Once out of their own special domain, the tension and'wildness' seemed to lessen considerably. We arrived safely in Puesto Paz, early afternoon, without any significant adventures."

FOR Anna the weekend was anything but easy. First there had been the hustle-bustle activity of getting the men off. Then suddenly, total quietness. Her co-worker, Faith, had a visitor, but Anna was alone, except for the Ayoré. The children had recently returned to school after their three month vacation, and now an empty hush hung over their places. Even with John around, Anna had felt the silence. Now with John out there at the battle front, the quiet was awesome and more than a little frightening.

After a radio contact with the men on Saturday, Anna and Faith radioed Tambo to report the message to the eight children — the Wienses' six and Paul and Faith's two. If worse came to worst the family should be forewarned. In either case the children ought to be informed and encouraged to join in special prayer. Anna's heart went out to them. The children seemed too young to bear so heavy a load. The contact man at the school informed her that "the children are taking it hard." She wished she could be with them; yes, to love them and hold them close. Instead she could only cling to his final words, "But they are praying earnestly. We are all praying with you."

The Ayoré were praying too. Without any white leadership they formed a prayer circle that continued twenty-four hours a day. One thought was uppermost. One of two things was going to happen — success or death. Only God knew which.

By Saturday night the tension in Anna had risen to a peak. The emptiness and uncertainty seemed simply too much. The question, "Is it worth it all?" began to torment her. She struggled for peace but as the darkness of the night enveloped her, the darkness in her own soul progressed in intensity.

"I can't give up my husband! It is too much, God." Forcefully, vehemently, the thoughts churned around within her. "I can't and I won't! . . . First let go of my children and then give up my husband! All for the sake of these ignorant, dirty, smelly . . . uh, forget it. That's not true either."

What should she do? She felt lost, and confused.

"Oh, God, I'm wrong. I know I'm wrong. I don't want to be like this," she began again. The worst rebellion was gone, but not the struggle. *I want Your way in my life. In John's life. In the children's lives. And yet . . . and yet . . . What shall I do? It's just too hard.*" Visions of those first five missionaries martyred in this very neighborhood danced before her eyes. The brutal, cruel killings. The long hopeless search for the survivors. The lonely widows and orphaned children struggling bravely to go on. "Oh, God, it cannot be. It cannot be Your will for us. No, you must not take John! God, I cannot let go! But . . . Lord, I want your way — why, why is it so hard?"

Slowly memories of past struggles came to her mind. She remembered the heat of the struggles, her kicking, fighting, God-resisting attitudes and then the peace that followed each time — the peace that is known only to those who experience the freedom of giving in to God. *Giving in to God.* Could it be? Was that her answer now? Was it time once more to surrender, to give in to God? Had she not done that already, and did that not suffice? Was she serving a God who always demanded more and more and more?

She struck a match, lit the faithful old kerosene lamp and picked up her Bible.

"Could you give me an answer or some kind of help through Your Word?" The prayer sounded listless and yet there was depth. She began to search. Suddenly the words began to stand out, to come alive. She was reading I Timothy 1:15.

"Christ Jesus came to the world to save sinners . . . *'Sinners, said Paul, like himself, like me, like these natives . . . .* 'For this cause I obtained mercy that in me first Jesus Christ might show all longsuffering, for a pattern to them which should hereafter believe.' *That's me! Paul left a pattern for me. And that's these natives. He left a pattern for them as well.* "This charge I commit unto thee . . . that thou mightest war a good warfare, holding faith and a good conscience . . .' *War a good warfare. Holding faith.*"

Suddenly she understood. The picture came into focus. She saw more clearly than ever before why Paul had said, "I die daily." Surrender had not been easy for him either. He had called the struggles 'war,' but he won the battles. The only way to lasting victory, the kind Paul had, was to renew those commitments again and again and again. Daily, he'd said. Could she expect less of herself?

"Lord, I accept Your will. Your will, not mine. And I know You will have a way for me and the children." Real peace settled in. Anna felt she could touch it, as if Jesus Himself had entered her room to help comfort her. "This joy is something I cannot find words to describe," she mused half aloud, as she blew out the light. The next thing she knew it was morning and time to radio the men. Even as she hurried to Faith's she remembered the overcoming peace. She knew it would last. No matter what, this was reality!

Little tremors, like the prelude to an earthquake, shook her when the message came through that afternoon, "A contact has been made." The tremors remained just that; a real quake never came. Her peace bounded right back and remained. Each time the radio reported safety, her faith was strengthened.

WHEN the trucks pulled in with the twenty-seven newcomers, an air of suspense, as well as very mixed feelings, prevailed. Just to be there and see it all was a tremendous experience for Anna.

To the jungle dwellers the change was most traumatic! Like innocent young children, they busied themselves with the art of exploring. To see, to touch, to feel was excitement in itself. Not only had they never experienced white men before but items like houses, doors, windows, dishes, spoons, etc., were completely foreign. They shot out questions about everything. Nervous shivers ran through Anna as she watched and listened. "These people are a strange mixture indeed. They live like animals, they think like children, but function like normal adults. Their inner self is all twisted up with superstition and cruelty, and yet they are souls that will live for all eternity. *What a challenge!*"

For John and Anna, being reunited was very special. Although the separation had lasted for only one long weekend, the preeminent danger had made it seem much longer. But now was not the time to reflect on that.

"I feel very sticky, filthy, in fact," John ventured shortly.

Anna hurried for towels and a clean change of clothes. What a pleasure to serve him! She could well imagine what it felt like to live without a shower for four days in this kind of heat.

While John showered, Anna got out the coffee pot. Soon the coffee was ready. The military commander, who had been watching outside, was ready for coffee, and some answers. Perhaps Anna could be just the right person to question.

"I don't understand this," he hesitantly began. Anna sensed his agitation. "Maybe you can explain it. I just don't understand how this can be. It's as if you have some special power or something. When we came in with soldiers, ammunition and back-up from the government, in a whole week we achieved nothing but more trouble. When you came in with only two white men, and no weapons, you persuaded, and won twenty-seven bloodthirsty savages within a day or two . . . *I simply can't understand it.*"

Anna longed for wisdom to answer him correctly. It was her opportunity to testify of her deep inner convictions. "You see, we serve God," she chose her words carefully. "It is *He*, not we, who has the special power. He has promised to give it to all those who serve Him. It's like His love. He has so much, He can generously supply all His followers." Warming up to her subject, she continued with confidence now. "Or you could say, it's like being enlisted in His army. We serve Him according to His rules and He helps us according to His power, which is awesome. He wants us to work for the welfare of the country too, and so it gives us real joy to be able to help out in a time of need such as this."

The room fell silent. The commander's eyes were fastened on her. His puckered brow spoke of puzzlement. Some of those thoughts were obviously very new to him, but his attitude said, "I'll be thinking about that for awhile yet." Without a word he quietly moved back outside. Anna was glad he had seen the whole thing. She was glad too that she could share with him a few words of their faith.

A news reporter came around to pick up the story. He was amazed as he gathered the details. His positive attitude showed itself in the well written story which hit the newspaper. Much credit was given to the mission as he explained its work and purpose.

In spite of these rewarding experiences, there were

behind-the-scene hassles that needed much wisdom and patience. Shortly after the arrival of the new group, two other residents, men who were still not believers, yelled, ''Let's kill 'em. Let's kill 'em.'' Quickly and firmly someone had to step in.

For the first number of days the tension in the whole village was very taut. Constant vigilance was needed to protect the peace and hopefully prevent actual war. John and Anna were amazed at the maturity of a number of their believers. With great adaptability they made themselves available. Much story-telling, counselling, prayer and midnight watching was given toward their new project. The effect was calming and good. Yet it was a whole month till everyone was settled down again, the twenty-four-hour-a-day vigilance could be dropped, and strangers could once more be allowed freely on site.

In the midst of this tense situation, Anna's inner peace had kept going and growing. When Paul Wyma said, ''God's angels must be busy, working overtime, first for the survey, then for the contact and now for the settling in,'' she heartily agreed. Now, as the tension eased, Anna could relax and rejoice in the thought, ''If God be for us, who can be against us?'' (Romans 8:31).

Chapter Twelve

THE PEOPLE came streaming in, truckload by truckload.
John and Paul kept up a hectic pace. Driving to the train
depot, picking up passengers, driving the 25 kilometers to the
mission, driving back, getting more passengers, driving, helping, driving . . . Excitement had been in the air for days, as
every inhabitant of Puesto Paz worked at the all-absorbing
task of getting ready. Finally the important day arrived! Excitement was at a feverish pitch! What was all this excitement
about? Why was everyone coming to Puesto Paz? This was the
Ayoré conference! The very first of its kind in Bolivia!
Ministers, deacons, wives and families, from five other stations, and representing almost as many mission organizations,
were to be there. For the people of Puesto Paz this was a
special honor. Not only were they the newest and smallest
settlement, but the believers there were the least in number
and the youngest in faith.

The Ayoré planned and conducted most of the services.
At dawn each day the week-long conference began with
prayer meetings. Immediately after breakfast they gathered
for the first service, and in the evening they held a second service. Both lasted for several hours and consisted of worship,
sharing and preaching.

As an opening part of the first several evenings Bob and
Ivy Hart from a different mission showed Spanish slides on
the life of Christ. This moved the people in a special way. By
the end of the week there were twenty-seven recorded decisions of persons having accepted Christ. On the last day they
held a beautiful baptism and communion service. John and
other missionaries present merely did the behind-the-scenes
guiding. What a blessing it was to see how well the Ayoré
were managing on their own!

For Anna, one little incident stuck out especially in her memory of that week. She and John had been participating until Thursday when the Harts needed a ride home and John had offered to take them. Alone at home that night, Anna decided to miss the service and get a little rest. She changed into pyjamas and sat down at their rough homemade table with a cup of cold coffee. Resting her head in her hands she realized how tired she was. Her body would appreciate this break.

Suddenly a slight noise startled her. She glanced up quickly. Oh no, a young man blocked the doorway! He just stood there looking at her. Anna froze with fright. She recognized him as one of the very recent Indian residents. What could he possibly want? And why hadn't he brought his wife? As she scrutinized him, Anna tried not to reveal her feelings. Tentatively she inquired, "Did you come for something? Is there something I can do for you?"

"I came to escort you safely to the meeting," came his decisive answer. Anna noted his totally sincere, guileless expression. What shame she felt immediately! With a sigh of relief she hurried to get ready. She dare not admit that she hadn't planned to go. It moved her to realize that this young man, a very new Christian, was doing this as a special effort to serve God. Having known of John's absence, he had planned this for her welfare. He had no inkling oa an impure thought. And to think, she hadn't trusted him!

THE general procedure for the local church called for services on Sundays, morning and evening, as well as Thursday nights. Although these were well attended, the Indian women had a problem which called for the ingenuity of the missionaries. They felt small, insecure and unequal beside their husbands. Their listening at services was accompanied with a shrug which said, "That's above my head. That deep stuff is good for the men. Now if there were something simple . . .

maybe . . . " Their attention remained shallow and aloof, like children listening in on adult lectures.

Anna and Faith began having special women's Bible studies on Friday nights. Here the women opened up, and revealed much keener perception. They grasped new truths and began the gigantic task of applying them to their own lives. This led to an increased desire to learn Scripture, which in turn led them to begin a Bible memory session on Wednesday nights. Anna enjoyed leading these, as verse after verse got tucked away with childlike enthusiasm.

JOHN had a knack for forming friendships and striking up conversation. Whether it was his Indian neighbors, or a government official, John spoke freely with either. He thoroughly enjoyed hearty discussions with Spanish-speaking nationals. One inevitable question came up frequently, a question that seemed most popular in the world at large, "Why are you trying to change these people?"

Several anthropologists had recently been asking this. One became quite dogmatic. "Man needs the security of his own culture and roots. You're disrupting their natural lifestyle and spoiling it with the demands of civilization. Right now the new ideas are a novelty to them, but eventually they will be left with no lifestyle to call their own. They will be left without pride, and without a culture."

"And," he continued emphatically, "the Ayoré have neither physical or emotional resistance to the diseases and problems of civilization, which you cannot help but bring with you. Are you actually ready to take responsibility for that? You know what I think? In your attempt to help the Ayoré, you are *greatly hindering* their welfare."

As Anna looked up, her eyes met John's. This accusation wasn't new, but it still hurt. They hadn't been taking the thought lightly either, for the memory of those awful measle epidemics were still seared on their minds. They knew there was some element of truth in the criticism, and yet there was another very important side to the issue. Together they had spent hours analyzing this very question, and their conclusion had always been the same.

With confidence John now replied, "Everyone needs a heritage and culture, I agree. But are we to let people continue in a culture that is extremely deficient? Are we to let them continue dying from poor eating and living habits just because they have a culture that we enjoy observing from the sidelines? How can we sit by idly when we know better?

"Anna and I are not out to change their lifestyle and ideas when they don't hinder health and happiness. But, when we know of ways to help them, aren't we selfish to keep that to ourselves? Most important, if we know of a peace and joy that comes only from having a personal relationship with Jesus Christ, Anna and I feel compelled to share it. Even if it means crossing cultural barriers!"

The anthropologist was not convinced.

John had an idea. "Let's ask one of them. Let them speak for themselves." There was no hesitation in the reply he received. Were the people sorry?

"No. No, never. We were very much unhappy. We very much afraid. Bird god bad. Evil spirits bad. We have no peace. But the missionaries came. They help us. Now we have peace. Now we happy, very much happy. We like."

When one of the native people did occasionally wander back into the jungle, he was sure to be back within a week with a new sense of appreciation.

To help the natives overcome their traditional fears and taboos, and experience instead the peace of God, was one task. No doubt it was more important than any other job, but without certain accompanying ones it was impossible. One of these was the art of learning acceptable standards of civilization. In its first basic form this hadn't caused a problem. The people were eager enough to enjoy such benefits as wearing clothes or having houses in which to live. But the deep underlying needs, although hard to put into words, were reason enough frequently to drive a man like John to his knees in prayer. It made him stretch his mind too, in search of resources and possible solutions.

The Ayoré were a nomadic people. Like wildlife, they had lived in and off the jungle, without any awareness of other possibilities. Now they had settled into a civilized community life. At first everything seemed wonderful, a bit like heaven. All too soon, however, the question of continuing support came up. The animal life around them had diminished rapidly once the people concentrated only on one area. Previously they had simply roamed to wherever they found wildlife, vegetation or anything to sustain them. Now that they had tasted the benefits of civilization, they suddenly became very aware of their need for money or some sort of trading system. And without special help, they just didn't know how to go about it.

John became deeply involved in this aspect of the work. Although the mission agency, the sponsors of Puesto Paz, had not always considered this of prime importance, John felt strongly that the evangelization success would deteriorate rapidly unless it was accompanied by some sort of answers for pressing daily problems. He felt that this was what James had meant when he said, "What does it profit? If a brother or sister be naked and destitute of daily food, and one of you say unto them, depart in peace, be ye warmed and filled, nothwithstanding ye give them not those things which are needful for the body, what doth it profit? Even so, faith if it hath not works, is dead, being alone." (James 2:14-17). To him that said, "Even so, if I try to be a missionary and don't apply myself to finding the answers to their problems, I might as well not be here."

Since the Ayoré were far from any public market, John put up a general store, which was open every second day for a couple of hours. In it he sold flour, sugar, rice, salt, coffee, tea, oil, matches, shoes, pots, bowls, spoons, scribblers, pencils and erasers. The Indians were no beggars. Every item was cheerfully paid for. However, the problem of where to raise the money became progressively bigger.

Some individuals had been working away from home for Bolivian employers, but there weren't enough jobs for everyone. Even those that did work often came back with multiple problems. The Indians tended to get cheated, discriminated against and sometimes outrightly abused. Because they were a small minority group, the Ayoré sensed little could be done.

A number spent their time weaving, an art learned during their jungle days. The beautiful, very colorful but artful decorated bags found ready markets. John and Anna were frequently astounded at the perfect beauty of the intricate designing. However, the weaving, besides the initial preparation of material, took a lot of time. Consequently, the income, although appreciated, did not go far.

John investigated further in attempts to alleviate the financial problems. He came home one day with an experimental project. He obtained three pigs from the University of Santa Cruz. These three, a sow ready to farrow, and two young ones, a male and a female, were the beginning of a farm. Patiently he introduced the project to his neighbors. Carefully he built a little corral for his 'farm', always showing just exactly what and why he was doing this. He had numerous curious, observant onlookers. He also found a nutritious type of grass which was a vast improvement over the previously grown squash or corn.

By the time the first litter of twelve lovely piglets had arrived, John had formulated his plans well. Each family could buy one young female pig from him and pay by giving him one of the firstfruits, a pig of like size from their first litter. It worked. They caught on and enjoyed the challenge. Although there were some drop-outs, before the end of their five-year term there were thirteen hog farmers in the little community. Each had paid for the initial pig. Each had built his own private corral and some were now raising as many as sixteen nice healthy pigs. The market for a finished pig was superb, so that this solution, while not eliminating the whole problem, was certainly a tremendous step forward.

Quite by accident another means of support was discovered. Anna became involved in working this one out. Apparently a good type of honeybee had escaped from Brazil and had decided to settle in the Puesto Paz area of Bolivia. Although the bee was mean and poisonous, it was an excellent producer. Unexpectedly the Ayoré found their jungle full of them. The natives would cut down a tree and find up to ten liters of honey inside. The honey was brought to Anna, who undertook the processing. For several years she was instrumental in selling or helping to sell about four hundred liters of clean sterile honey. The five-liter containers went fast, and the income was a real help, but for Anna this meant a great deal of extra work.

"John," Anna started one evening, after a particularly hectic day, "I'm just so tired I feel like asking, 'Why?' Oh, I know why we're here and all that, and really I'm glad. But sometimes it would be so nice just to relax, or visit a friend, or even go shopping leisurely." Involuntarily, a long sigh escaped her.

John squeezed her hand gently. No words were needed. He understood better than she realized.

"Oh dear," Anna admonished herself, "I should be ashamed. John probably works much harder than I and I haven't even considered how tired he must be sometimes. Anyway, we are in this together and I have no business getting depressed." When she remembered the vast difference between the 'then' and 'now' of their people, her attitude changed rapidly.

"Remember when they used to survive for long periods of time on a simple fruit like the 'sepoe'," John would recall. That was a fruit-vegetable, similar to watermelon, white and fairly firmly textured. With its moist contents, it had provided a meager means of survival when the people had run out of both food and water.

"The change is well worth some extra effort," Anna acknowledged thoughtfully.

"Isn't it ever." John's ready response came heartily.

AFTER the completion of their home, for which John had given many hours of loving labor, he soon began construction of a school. A simple but fair-sized structure made of local wood, was soon completed. It became a monument of the new life in the community. The furniture included benches and tables. The tables were long, sturdy oldfashioned tables, with tuck-in shelves underneath. The benches were attached firmly at certain places. Such furniture needed to be heavy and well attached to avoid problems with 'long fingers.'

Having undisciplined children remained a problem. When parents became conscious of this problem, they would pray. When they found that even long, loud, persistent prayers didn't make their children good, they were totally stumped. If God couldn't do it, who could? The idea of consistent teaching, training and disciplining was totally foreign to them. When a missionary tried to teach the concept they seemed to form a mental block. The thought was much too strange!

The new school had ten benches, each seating about six students comfortably. In 1979 their enrollment stood at sixty-three, ages five to twelve. Culture still demanded that as soon as a teenager entered puberty he or she was ready to marry, settle down, and be an adult. No school was needed for any teenager.

FOR John and Anna's family, their missionary lifestyle called for more than cultural adjustments. The physical adjustments provided repeated adventures. Snakes, scorpions, and tarantulas constantly offered a variety of experiences. But even these were not the only offenders.

Monica awoke one night with a start. "Help!" she screamed, "There's something crawling in my bed!" A light couldn't be found fast enough. It didn't take long to discover the culprits. Their cat had caught a rat and obviously wished to proceed with a feast in Monica's bed! Monica grabbed the cat in one hand and the now dead rat by the tail in the other, and hurled them both outdoors in disgust.

"You can celebrate there," she fairly hissed to the cat, as she closed the door ever so firmly.

"You *always* shake out all things before using," someone had told them at the very start. That rule proved very relevant. If someone forgot to shake the towel before drying himself he might well be bitten by a scorpion or centipede.

On one occasion, before putting on her walking shoes to go out, Anna proceeded to shake them well. When slipping her foot into the second shoe, she thought, "Wow! I didn't know that the insole was loose and crumpled." She took the shoe off and stuck in her hand to straighten things out. Before Anna could grasp the situation, a huge tarantula, merely humiliated from the squashing, was walking arch-backed up her arm! Without thought but rather by instant reflex, Anna swiped at the creature. Off it flew, before it had a chance to bite.

"Thank you, Lord, for protecting me," came through a number of times in her prayer that night. Bites from this type of tarantula frequently produced long-term problems. Was Anna ever glad and thankful! She didn't really need any more problems.

A group of four unexpected guests, had arrived just before dinner. While John and the children took them on a tour of the village, Anna prepared the meal. Suddenly she sighted a poisonous snake, an adder, in a bedroom.

"Here I am all by myself," she reasoned calmly. "I'll tell John at dinner. In the meantime I'll just close that door tightly."

When the group came in to eat, Anna promptly forgot about the snake. Later when they took the guests to the airstrip she was too preoccupied to remember a snake. Even when John took the boys on the swamp buggy on an errand to the train depot 25 kilometers away, she didn't remember.

At bedtime, she stepped outside for a moment to observe the lightning. "That always reminds me of snakes seeking shelter whenever a thunderstorm approaches . . . oh no, the snake!" Suddenly she remembered! The snake was still in the bedroom! Her three girls were all in that very bedroom totally unaware.

She rushed inside. After peering into the room, and seeing no immediate cause for alarm, she called in a hoarse whisper, "Girls, I have something to tell you." Although sleepy and puzzled, the girls hurried to mother's side. What could she want at this hour? It must be important. After a little consultation they hastily formed their battle line. Rachel took the light while Anna took the lance. The twins followed close behind cautiously searching everywhere. Systematically, inch by inch, they went through every corner, nook and cranny. Suddenly, there it was! Under the bottom of the bookshelf, curled up tightly in the dark corner, there sat the unsuspecting snake!

The battle began and ended rapidly! It was with a feeling of pride and accomplishment that they held up the dead snake and told their story.

Never once during the whole five years did Anna treat any of her family or fellow missionaries for snake bite, nor, for that matter, any other serious bites. "Maybe sometime in the future, it will be God's will for us to suffer from snake bite," she confided to a friend. "But in the meantime, it's really a canopy, a canopy of love, that God is holding over us to keep us safe."

The psalmist once said, "He will not suffer thy foot to be moved, He that keepeth thee will not slumber" (Psalm 121:3) and that certainly had been holding true.

"HEY, John, don't you think you should call the children? It's way past their usual bedtime," Anna inquired, shivering. The book she was reading just couldn't hold her attention any longer.

John got up and adjusted the lamp. It always demanded attention. "Oh leave 'em be. It's not every day they have so much fun," he returned, as he went to sit down right beside her. Did he sense perhaps that she needed a little extra support? Anna snuggled closer and felt John's warmth and strength. Together they relaxed quietly, enjoying each other's closeness without needing to speak.

Together they listened to the racket outside. Laughter and boisterous chatter filled the air, for all the young Wienses and a number of native children were playing Hide and Seek. The full moon had attracted them, and the fun had reached such a fervor, they could have played all night.

Finally Anna broke the stillness inside. "John, think of all the poisonous snakes outside. The children might step on them. They haven't even got a flashlight."

No answer.

"But what if some wild Indians should be snooping around like they sometimes do? In the bright moonlight our children would make excellent material for target practice."

No answer.

"JOHN!"

Slowly he arose. He hated to break the feeling of comfortable ease. And, he hated to break into the enjoyment of the youngsters. But, yes, maybe Anna was right. Maybe he better call them in.

"SQUASH again," whined Rachel.

"Yeah, squash on Monday, squash on Tuesday, squash on Wednesday, squash on . . ."

"Or purple sweet potatoes. That's the worst."

"No-o. Oatmeal porridge seven days a week is the worst."

"Oh, for some good Canadian food." That one came like a wail.

John listened silently to the thankless chatter. Suddenly his measure was full, his mind made up. Rapping his hand sharply on the wooden table, he called for attention and laid down the law.

"There will be no more grumbling here. Absolutely none!" He sounded very decisive. After a pause (it was so quiet you could hear a pin drop) he continued, a little more gently, "God has been so good to us by supplying us with food, any food. And we must thank Him for it — not complain like the Israelites did so often in the desert. This business of grumbling must be stopped absolutely before it becomes a habit. For a start, and I mean starting right now, anyone caught complaining will be chosen to lead aloud in a prayer of thanksgiving for that very same meal."

"And so we learned not to grumble," reported Rachel later.

"No, we just learned to postpone it till after the prayers were finished," corrected Monica mischievously.

"AH shucks, Daddy, you *always* win," sighed Freddie, as he got up to put the crokinole board away. "But then," he told himself, "I shouldn't worry. Daddy even beat Arthur the other night. Albert too, I think."

He sauntered over to his brothers. The two had been waging a long and royal war with a game of chess. It looked as if Arthur would win. He usually did.

Game nights at home were fun — such a pleasant break from school. If only he could win at least *one* game. Restless, he turned back to John.

"Let's wrestle, Daddy," he coaxed. John couldn't resist. Down on the floor they went, rolling, twisting, tangling. Soon every other game in the room came to a halt as the players joined together in the grandstand.

"Get him, Freddie, get him!"

"Come on Freddie, you can do it."

Encouragement came from every side as the youngsters cheered on their hero. John relaxed his hold just a little, and Freddie made quick use of the moment. With one quick, powerful lunge, he had the upper hand. Gasping, as if for air, John sputtered, "I . . . guess . . . you've got me."

"Say, 'surrender,' Daddy, say you surrender!"

"I surrender," John's voice sounded absolutely genuine.

After a round of applause and fervent claps on the back from big brother, Freddie went to bed as a victor. He had *won!*

Slyly Anna whispered, "Thanks, John, he needed that."

John just winked at her, suppressing the telltale smile. Then he turned and said gruffly, "Let's get to bed, Anna."

AFTER a consultation with their new doctor, John and Anna realized that Anna would need surgery to remove her gall bladder. This was in 1978 and their funds were very low. They felt a special longing for more prayer and financial support. Only a few months later the picture changed. Extra money had come in, they felt the needed support, and were ready to go ahead. "Isn't it amazing how God works? Thousands of miles away people are moved to give and pray just when we need it most," Anna remarked as she readied herself. That thought helped quench the secret fears that lurked inside her. Was there a possibility that a doctor's optimism would prove to be correct at least once and she wouldn't experience all sorts of emergency hassles?

The surgery did turn out to be another major emergency. A brand new kind of anesthetic was used which worked fine. Anna showed no negative reaction. The doctor, however, knowing of her multiple allergies, had decided to proceed with multiple surgeries now rather than subject Anna to another operation in the near future. Besides removing her gall bladder, the doctor removed a cyst, one ovary and fixed a hernia.

151

She could not tolerate any pain killers and shortly after 'coming around' started going into shock. The medical staff kept a close watch. When the doctor noticed Anna going into shock he sprang into action. Every effort was made to rouse her.

"Don't give up," he pleaded. "Just don't give up."

She did not respond. She could not.

All efforts seemed of no avail. Finally the doctor in desperation, sat down beside her to offer encouragement. "It's not that bad. It's not really bad at all. Anna, you have done so well. Please Anna, respond!"

What could she do? She heard him but could not exert enough effort to open her eyes. Even when she tried, they refused to cooperate. She could feel herself floating, floating away into space. Was this what dying felt like?

After what seemed a long time, the voices that had been blurry and faraway suddenly cleared. She recognized the doctor's voice again. This time it was loud, vehement. He sounded desperate. "Don't be a chicken," she heard him say. To whom was he speaking, and what did he mean? He said it again. Was he teasing?

"Don't be so chicken." Suddenly her mind cleared one step further. Chicken? Was she chicken? That was funny. She couldn't help it. She laughed aloud. Her laughter brought a sigh of relief. This was what he wanted. He expected this to be the turning point. It was. Her blood pressure started going back to normal, her pulse grew stronger and some color returned to her face. Very soon the critical stage was over and she began to recover more rapidly.

On the eleventh day she was able to fly home. What joy to be home again. And, what a pleasure — to be able to eat anything again. For almost two years her diet had consisted mainly of honey and crackers.

She had been home for three days but still felt weak and tired. She decided to retire early for the night. At nine o'clock there was a couple at the window. The young woman was in premature labor. Help was needed. Would Anna please come?

Could she do it? Could she go and spend the night working? Anna did not know. Even as she got up, a wave of nauseating dizziness overcame her. She would need a miracle. Quickly she and John prayed for strength, then together they ventured out. As she went she could feel the utter tiredness leave her and new strength flow through her. The asked-for miracle had come.

At two in the morning a little boy was born, weighing almost three pounds. Wishing for an incubator, Anna struggled with the tiny baby for several hours before concluding that he might live. Appreciating the special challenge, she prayed for success. Under the old ways such a baby would have been buried alive at once. Now things were different. The parents were interested in going God's way. Would He bless their effort and have it work out?

The baby was breathing normally at last and Anna praised the Lord for victory. Finally she could return to her own bed. When she lay down for a belated rest, she once again committed the youngster to God. She was convinced that God was in this. Everything would work — the baby would live.

As she relaxed before drifting off to sleep, she sensed a song in her heart. She wanted to shout it aloud, but she was too tired. Inside, however, the song was very real.

"He giveth more grace as the burdens grow greater,

He giveth more strength as the labors increase . . .

He giveth . . . more . . ."

She awoke with a smile. The thoughts had stayed with her. God did give strength! She remembered the comment Paul had once made, "When I am weak, then am I strong." How true that was!

"Isn't it great that we can serve a God like that?" she whispered to no one in particular as she rose to face what was left of the day.

A FIVE- year term can seem very long especially when

breaks or breathers are very sparse. Sometimes John and Anna's work and responsibilities loomed like a mountain range with no end in sight.

At such times, when the horizon seemed dismal and the zest would run low, the appearance of guests could brighten the day. Tourists, seemingly from all over the world, would choose Puesto Paz as a place to visit. No doubt the improved airstrip and the fact that it was only a half-hour flight from Santa Cruz had much to do with this.

Since her family was gone so frequently, Anna revelled in the idea of preparing pleasant family-sized meals. The unexpectedness however often sent her scurrying. She needed the Seven-Eleven or Mini-Mart. But none was around! She needed a stock of easy-to-do, prepared-beforehand foods. But that was impossible! But who cared? Even when done the long, hard way, Anna's meals were attractive and nourishing. Such days turned out to be a joy and encouragement. They felt more like a Sunday than any other day. What joy, what happiness, what fulfilment! If only these times would last a little longer.

One such tourist family seemed especially dear to Anna. How she longed to find time to share her heart! But it was not to be. Before they left the woman turned to Anna and asked kindly, "How are you really? . . . Are you happy here?" What an opportunity to unburden! But, alas, there was time only for the expected "fine" and "wonderful," and then they too were gone!

Anna wiped away a stray tear. She certainly could not afford to dabble with self-pity. That would never do. That night, however, she spent a lot of time thinking. The pleasant tourist visits all turned out very much the same. The group or couple would get an interesting tour of the village, would ask a lot of questions, take a number of pictures, enjoy a hearty meal and then be gone. As surely and abruptly as the smiling faces appeared, they vanished again.

Anna was puzzled. What was missing? Why did she feel let down? She could not understand what was missing, she knew only that something was needed. Suddenly she recognized it! Her conclusion was so clear she felt an urge to shout it from the housetops.

"I know!" she told herself fiercely. "I'm starved for love and fellowship and interchange with people like me. The people here — no matter how much I love them — are still like little children. They're like a large family of young, lovely, always needy children, but I have a need to stretch my mind and spirit with adults like myself once in awhile. Just as Mary listened at Jesus' feet, just as Americans go to conventions, seminars and workshops to learn and experience new truths, fresh food, so I too need refreshing and newness. Our life is made up so largely of giving and giving. No wonder our well sometimes wants to run dry.

"If our visitors knew of this, I believe they would help. We could sit, talk, and maybe, share our hearts. If they had time and cared enough to listen, why, I could tell them where it's really at! I could share my real needs, problems and frustrations. Then I would listen to them share theirs. Together we might search for answers. Together we could pray, and thank God for all the latest victories."

Her heart was full as she shared this with John.

His spontaneity refreshed her. "Oh Anna, what wonderful insights. How true, how very true. Let's tell the visitors and maybe things can change for the better."

"In the meantime," determined Anna a little later," I will thank God for his presence. It is not like someone said, 'When I have no one talk to, I talk to the wall. It helps too.' Instead of that wall, I have God. He is real and alive and personally interested."

She forced herself to hang tough and shelve her desires for the moment. She prayed, "Thank you, Lord, for meeting my need when there is no one else. Thank you . . . I know in your own time you will send answers to all my needs, even human answers. Thank you, Lord."

Paul had spoken well the deep truths she was trying to

learn. "I have learned in whatever state I am, therewith to be content. I know how to be abased and how to abound . . . to be full or to be hungry . . . to abound or to suffer needs. I can do all things through Christ which stengthens me" (Phil. 4:11-13).

"Isn't it a blessing to know we're not the first ones on this road?" Anna pondered aloud.

"Nor are we the last," John murmured softly. With those reassuring thoughts they fell asleep full of thankfulness and peace inside.

Chapter Thirteen

THE BURDEN of the work had been lying heavily on Anna's heart. During some of John's absences, she had to carry on alone. Other workers frequently had to move around. It seemed that none stayed at Puesto Paz as regularly as the Wienses. Surely this was all part of God's will. Lately one aspect of the work had become especially heavy on Anna's mind. The years were slipping by and their five-year term was coming to a close. Had they accomplished what they had set out to accomplish? Were the results, great as they were, the size of God's intention? What about all the needs that were still unmet? Would there be someone to pick up after them?

At the women's meetings Anna had frequently counselled on what she would term "The Christian Home." Feeling that this area was one of the very greatest needs, she put all her imagination and effort into it. When the women became true believers they changed a lot. They wanted to be good wives and mothers. They wanted healthy, loving, obedient children, and sometimes they succeeded surprisingly well. On other occasions the traditional superstitions and long-standing cultural habits just took over and played havoc with all of Anna's careful teaching. Her heart would ache with disappointment and frustration. When would these dear people grow up and be able to remember lessons? Would the tender young plants never form deep roots?

On one occasion Anna and her daughters were home alone during vacation, when a mother came running with a desperate plea for help. "My son is trying to kill me. My son wants to kill me," she screamed.

Anna couldn't believe it. *That son was ten years old!* Surely he wouldn't kill his mother. Anna glanced outside and saw the excited mob. Right in the middle stood the boy, looking very angry indeed. Maybe she had better check things out!

She rushed out to get a closer look. The mother followed, or so Anna thought. Suddenly, as if out of nowhere, she saw the mother charge at her son with an upraised axe in her hand. There was a jerk and a swish! Quick as a whistle, the boy was gone! He had no intentions of having himself chopped into pieces.

Several of the bystanders laughed loudly. The mother angrily vowed to get the boy as soon as he returned. She kept her axe ready. Anna felt weak and shaken. What should she do? *That mother was a professing Christian.*

It turned out that the boy remained in the jungle till the following day when his father came home to protect him and iron out the mess. Outwardly the problem appeared solved, but in both John's and Anna's hearts a burden remained. They needed a lot of patience and understanding. Fiery outbreaks, like hangovers from jungle savagery, occurred frequently. When these involved a Christian, it was likely that he'd repent within the hour and, like Peter in the Easter story, go out and weep bitterly. He'd ask, "Why was I so angry? I didn't want to be like that." Yet it tended to happen again and again.

There were other problems with the Ayoré families. The cultural mores dictated that when a marriage broke up, the children of that marriage had to be killed. The missionaries had tried earnestly to void that custom, and lately such parents would at least consider offering those children to the grandparents.

On one occasion this problem left Anna dumbfounded. A beautiful young mother had come to her with a rather sick three-month-old baby. Fearful lest her baby die, she had murmured loving phrases to it and wept in concern. Everything about the relationship looked very good. Lovingly Anna nursed the baby back to health. Joy and optimism had reigned although the mother and her husband were not yet

Christians.

Two weeks later the man deserted his wife. In stark desolation, with fixed face and coldly staring eyes, the mother ran and threw her child into the jungle. Fortunately someone saw her and followed to pick up and perhaps adopt the baby. When efforts were made to let the mother change her mind, she turned away resolutely. Without batting an eye she denied having any love for the child.

Anna felt her heart would break. Such a lovely mother and child. How could it be? Sometimes it seemed the Ayoré, in their final struggle about accepting a new faith, clung more desperately than ever to the traditional rules. Tradition demanded "Throw the baby out to die. Do not show your feelings. Do not weep when you suffer." The poor mother had hung on very faithfully. She had nothing better. Even when an aging grandmother tried vainly to nurse the child, and the child deteriorated until it eventually died, the mother showed no further emotion. To her the child had been dead the day she tossed it into the jungle.

"We will have to make even greater efforts to reach all of our people," Anna determined. "When they really accept Christ, they demonstrate a radical change. And yet . . . and yet there are still so many who have not responded. Oh that they would see the light! Would they come soon?"

During services or other sharing times the problems did not seem as big. Instead, these events often were a time of victory, a time of spiritual reaping. The victories seemed more noticeable.

John became aware of these victories during a Bible study as he conversed with some believers. Three had recently accepted Christ. "How do you like the Word of God?" John asked.

Their answer was heart-warming. "We like," they agreed confidently. "It is sweet like honey. We like what you teach. We like the Father's Word. It is sweet in our stomach. But we cannot understand all the direction it takes."

"What a challenge!" John told Anna later. "If only there would always be someone around to show them that direction."

Although sharing at the services was a common practice, the young fellows were hesitant because they just might be laughed to scorn by those who weren't in it yet. Religion, after all, was most suitable for older folks. Anna's sympathy was really aroused one time when a young fellow, just barely in his teens, got up to share his newfound joy in the Lord. The booing and jeering got out of hand, and the young fellow ran to hide under a blanket beside his mother.

Somehow it registered in the hearts of these people that a genuine conversion experience entailed a long elaborate confession of every wrong ever committed. While this has some merit, the overemphasis it received caused the missionaries some concern. They soon tried to curb the practice. Such was, after all *not* a scriptural requisite for faith or assurance of salvation.

Yet, the concept of confessions remained with the people. It seemed a part of their make-up. When a person wanted to tell of his commitment to Christ for the first time, a detailed story of his life was the expected thing. One such service Anna could not forget. The service was perhaps halfway through when an old man, a hardened warrior and one-time chief, suddenly got up. He spoke out clearly, with deep feeling. Everyone listened. *When someone is directed by the Spirit to speak up in church, you must pay attention.*

"Now I must say something. Our ways are very bad. When we were in the jungle we were very bad. We had no good. I want the New Life. I want God. I have learned I was very wrong, but I change. I will follow God's way." Tears choked him up for a moment before he continued. "One time we were in the jungle. We saw four Bolivians riding horseback. Two had guns, two did not. We watched. I say, 'Let's shoot the two men who have guns, and the two horses whose riders don't have guns.' We shoot like I say. The other

160

two horses run away, and the two men very scared. They try to run away, but we run after. We let them run a little and then we stab them a little. Run a little more and stab a little more. Finally they fall down, fold their hands and call very earnestly. We did not understand. Now I think maybe they prayed to God. Maybe they prayed to us to let them live. I do not know. But we were very bad. We stabbed them more. At last we killed them. We said it was a good sport. We did many such things."

Deep sobs escaped him from somewhere inside. The others sat in a holy hush. All understood that he was reliving the hellish experience in minute detail. Many others were probably doing the same. Finally he regained his composure and continued with conviction. "Now we know better. We have heard God's Word, like it has been taught. I will choose, I now choose to follow Jesus. He is God's Son. He died to make me free. He is my Redeemer, and I will be His child."

A mighty hush hung over the audience after he sat down. Many eyes were moist. Hearts were moved. There was no doubt in anybody's mind — the thing they'd heard was real. It would make a difference, a mighty difference, both now and for all eternity.

Anna was too moved for words. Later, when sleep refused to come she lay awake and meditated on the event. "If Satan, or anyone, ever tempts me again with the question, 'Is it worth it?' I just wish I could give him a recording of that story. It seems incredible that anyone ever thought it was not worth it." She thanked God for the opportunity to be part of this story.

There were other memorable services. One day an Ayoré minister was preaching vehemently. Unexpectedly he looked at the missionaries in the back row. His voice changed from vehemence to tenderness. Without warning the theme of his message changed. "I cannot understand *why* the white men have come. They have homes. I have not seen their homes, but I know they are nice, very nice. They have mothers and

161

fathers, sisters and brothers, friends and churches and schools. They have left it all to come here. I cannot understand, but I know they love God and they love us. And I am happy, very happy that they have come. Aren't you? We must all thank God. We must tell God we are very happy."

John had been wishing for an opportunity to form another survey team in search of more groups of the still wild and wandering nomads. However, each time he thought he could see his way through he was swamped with other work as more emergency requests came in to demand his attention. One day he simply put it before the Lord. "When the time is ripe, when You want me to go, Lord, please just nudge me. Let me know . . ." He trusted, knowing that God would show him. With that assurance he could go back to his many other tasks.

One special need that weighed heavily on his mind now needed greater attention. *The village had no church building.* Outdoor services generally were no problem and certainly fitted right in with the culture of the people. The missionaries, however, because they always reflected on other possibilities, could not appreciate the inconveniences. When it rained all services would be cancelled. In the hot season, the services would be held at dawn before the sweltering heat became unbearable. In wet seasons the people would find themselves sitting right in the mud puddles during the service. Besides helping to solve all these problems, a church building would also teach stability and unity.

When the decision to build was made, John became deeply involved. Not only did he take over the leadership of the project, but together with several Ayoré believers, he worked hard, at the expense of sore muscles and long hours. From trees to sawmill, from sawmill to the building site, the jobs moved. Slowly the building went up. When it was finally completed the workers could look at it with pride and a feeling of accomplishment. Wasn't it the nicest Ayoré church around? It certainly was the biggest one to date. The frame building, finished on the outside with lovely cedar wood, the tin roof and shutters on the windows ready to close when needed, were all important parts of the new building. Then came the next phase — the building of the benches. When these were done the church could comfortably seat two hundred people.

The people loved their church. "The way they express their thanks and appreciation makes me feel rewarded," John commented to Anna one night. "It certainly makes up for all the aches, pains and sweat."

THEN, almost before John and Anna knew it, it was time to leave. Because, they were so attached to the people, the thought of leaving seemed impossible. However John and Anna realized that they and the children needed a break. Furlough would be good for them.

The date was set. John booked flights for June 11, 1980, and trusted that the funds would come in. They watched and waited but when no funds came, the flight had to be cancelled. Arthur, their oldest son, who had preceded them to Canada after graduating from high school, phoned. "Why didn't you come?" was his puzzled question. He couldn't believe their explanation! "But, the church here in Manitoba sent you prepaid tickets long ago." Arthur continued. "You mean you never received them?"

What now? Where was the hold-up? Was Satan playing havoc with their plans or did God have something better in store for them?

Their patience was wearing thin. Here it was the fifteenth, four days after their planned departure and they were still in Santa Cruz. The family was driving through the city when without warning a motorcycle came up from a side road, failed to stop, and swerved crazily right into their lane. What now? The heavy traffic forced them to stay in that same lane. John slammed on the brakes, but had no chance! *Bang! Boom! Crash!* Midst gasps and screams of horror from his

163

family, John brought the truck to a full stop.

The hurt man, probably in his late fifties, had obviously been drunk. When they had him safely in the hospital they breathed a sigh of relief. Everything was again in order so they thought. But a new, greater problem developed which made them forget all about the accident. The police officers at the scene took note of the situation. They rushed to find John and Anna. Everyone was ordered to the station.

Apparently an anti-American revolt had just begun. This accident was ample ground to catch those awful Americans. "But we're Canadians," John insisted, to no avail. They must be Americans, and must be punished. John was taken to prison, the truck was confiscated, Anna and the children were questioned before being allowed to go to the mission house.

The revolt seemed to follow them. All around there were shootings, bombings and explosions. This commotion continued all night. There was absolutely no possibility for sleep. Would their building be attacked next, or would God answer their earnest pleas for protection?

Morning finally came! And with it came the awful news. The American Consulate had been bombed and totally ruined.

"But there's much reason to thank God," said one of the men. "The American ambassador was out, and no one was hurt." That day only Canadian workers dared answer the telephone. To the oft-repeated questions in regard to searching out the Americans, they could staunchly answer, "I am a Canadian," and leave it at that.

Everyone was warned to stay at home. Warnings came repeatedly that no one was to go on the streets. The killings were numerous and the shootings were totally unpredictable.

For John the days became a nightmare. What a miserable existence in a dingy cell. He remembered Paul in his frequent imprisonments and knew that confidence in God and His promises was the only light ahead. Periodically John was allowed to visit his family at the mission house, but he had to make sure he returned promptly at the appointed time.

First he, then Anna, contacted a lawyer, a good friend of John's. The lawyer managed to get him out for a little while, but it did not last. "He's a spy," the officers would say. "He's one of Carter's right-hand men."

On the twenty-second Arthur phoned to check if the tickets had arrived. Anna's subdued answer of "Yes, but Daddy's in jail," choked him up. In a stunned voice he concluded the strained conversation, "We'll pray, Mom. We'll pray." These words lingered long with Anna. She knew the whole church would join him.

Because there appeared to be no change in sight, Anna and the children went back to Puesto Paz. The outward signs of revolution had quieted down, but John's release seemed far away. It was only by faith that they could proceed but their faith was mingled with tears and frustrations. Physically they were spent from the suspense of not knowing. Surely God had not forgotten them. Would they find, perhaps at a later date, that He had a real purpose behind all this?

In the midst of their questioning, John radioed to Anna, "It looks very hopeless here. Please leave as planned without me."

"But we need you," Anna argued. "I need you. The children need you. *We can't go without you.* And I'm sure you don't want to stay there alone."

He kept insisting. Numbly, Anna began to think of doing that, yet the whole thing didn't seem real. Wasn't God's answer going to come through at all? Would it come too late?

"Oh, schucks," she admonished herself. "Here I go worrying again. Surely Jesus would say to me, 'Oh, ye of little of faith.' I'll just have to commit it all to God and be happy either way."

It wasn't easy. By now the native neighbors all knew the situation. Their weeping was most pathetic. It had been bad enough to think of John and Anna's leaving, but to realize that their beloved Don Juan was imprisoned was unthinkable.

They clamored pitifully around Anna, trying to give comfort and yet needing it so badly themselves.

The days of waiting and wondering were running out. Something would have to give. In utter weariness Anna threw herself on her bed, wishing for oblivion. If only she knew with assurance what she ought to do. In utter helplessness she handed the mess to the Lord. "You do with us as You will." With that she fell soundly asleep.

Anna awoke with a start. Was it hours ago or only a few minutes since she fell asleep? What was all the chatter and commotion? More trouble? No, this sounded joyous. Arousing quickly, she stuck her head out of the door to inquire about it. "John's coming. John's coming," someone yelled.

It couldn't be! But sure enough, there he was! It was true! John was out of jail, and he was here walking toward her. It struck her as uncanny. Maybe this was what the disciples felt when they suddenly saw Jesus walking on the water toward them in the midst of the storm.

"How did it all happen? What made them change their minds? Didn't you get time to radio us? Is the revolt over? Are you free for good?" The questions were thrown at John.

John chuckled. "To all of your questions, the answer is 'I don't know.' There is no real explanation; only God knows. I'm convinced it is a direct miraculous answer to prayer."

"But how did it happen?"

"Yes, tell us about it, Dad."

"Well," began John, "It's a long story, and I'm not sure that any of it makes sense. One day I was in a teasy mood, and I told the officers, 'If you don't let me go, I'll get my family to join me. We could live in this cell together.' With a hint of sarcasm, the officer responded, 'And then what would you do? Evangelize all of us in here?'

" 'Exactly,' I told him, still in a light vein. 'If need be, that's exactly what we'd do.'

"I must have struck a sensitive nerve. The officer left, deep in thought.

"Yesterday I overheard some of the officers talking about me. They referred to me as 'that dumb American.' So I confronted them. How many times hadn't I told them *I was a Canadian?* This time for some reason, they believed me. After that . . . well, all of a sudden they just let me go."

THE flight home was perfect, right on schedule.

"I wonder if we'll ever know why all these things happened," Anna mused as they were sitting back to relax and enjoy the stretch of beautiful scenery whizzing by so far below them. "I mean all those if's . . . if the tickets had come for the first scheduled flight . . . if the drunk motorcyclist hadn't blocked our path . . . if the revolution hadn't been on exactly that day . . . if . . . if . . . if. Wouldn't this all have been so different?" There was no edge of complaint in her voice; she was simply thinking aloud and wondering.

It was a moment or two before John was ready with an answer. Even then he was deeply thoughtful. "One thing we have to remember. By serving the Lord in this way we are actually fighting on a battlefront, seeking to conquer Satan's territory. Soldiers on the front line are more likely to get shot at than those who back them up from behind. It's not that the place is more important. Without good back-up we could never even go, but physically at least it's more dangerous. Remember the time we went to contact the group of wild Ayoré? The danger was extremely great. Satan and his host of helpers are not at all interested in having us advance or make progress in whatever they considered his territory. Yet," he paused, and continued with greater emphasis, "in spite of that and even if we never know all the reasons, I am convinced the experience was rich and meaningful. Now that it is over, I know I will never regret it."

FURLOUGH is always a special time for missionary families. Special for seeing friends and family, special for reporting to the various individuals and churches that have supported them and special for receiving a much needed break and a time of refreshing. But to John and Anna, it was special in more ways than that.

Their family was growing up, and while actually enjoying that, they realized that as far as their missionary career was concerned it put them at a crossroad. Should they stay home till their children were all settled down, as some families were doing? Did God's call still come first or was it the family now? Shouldn't there be a way that one could combine both, without failing either?

Arthur had already made plans for his future, which included a job, aviation training and Bible school. That was fine. Albert was planning to go back with them to help with the Indian work, and return later to further his own training. But Rachel — and this is what hit Anna hard — was hoping to stay on alone to finish her grade twelve and then work.

"I can't bear the idea, John. She is so young and seems so fragile. I feel as if I should stay around to protect her."

"I know what you mean, Anna . . . And yet, she's exactly as old as you were when I married you."

Anna did not answer. She could find no answer. Her heart was too heavy to talk much that night.

Once again they brought their need before God, and waited on Him for answers. For days on end, things kept getting worse instead of better. Guilt crept in and haunted Anna.

"Why, now that the children are starting to leave, I see all the mistakes I've made as a mother. I've been impatient. I've been unkind. I've been too strict, and sometimes too lenient. I haven't taken nearly enough time to listen, to understand them, to train them thoroughly . . ." The list was endless.

One day she felt totally fed up with herself and her negative thoughts. "I desperately need something, God. I don't know what, but please help me." It was then that it struck her. Why, these inner accusations and worries were a direct attack of Satan. He didn't want her back on the mission field!

That revelation put a new light on the whole subject. With new determination she began to fight the discouragement for what it was, and soon began feeling much better.

One night while sharing with friends, John described it this way. "It's like putting weights on an old-fashioned balancing scale. On the one side you have the known will of God. On the other you have your own will with its natural, and often, selfish desires. The battle we face lies in choosing which weight, or which side of the scales, will win . . . But the more I consider it, the less glamor there is in going my own way."

Inevitably people would question them, sometimes very pointedly, "You mean you really are going back?"

To Anna, answering this was never easy. Her emotions were too involved, and the prospect of saying goodbye to her children brought much distaste, although she could face the prospect more positively now. She recognized that one by one, her loved ones would leave home, but she, as long as she were able, must remain, together with her husband, at her place in God's service. In whatever ways she could, she would lovingly help and support her children, but never at the expense of disobeying God.

One day while explaining this, she was so moved, she suddenly burst into tears. Through the tears she continued, "But I know without a doubt, that there's no place in the whole world I'd rather be, than exactly where God puts me. As long as I live, and God gives me grace, that is where I want to be."

Whenever John was questioned about a possible return he would answer very briefly, "Yes, we are going back. Wouldn't you?" And then he'd whip out a yellow card from the pack he carried in his shirt pocket, and pass it on.

Would You?
If you had been to heathen lands
Where weary souls stretch out their hands
To plead, yet no one understands,

169

Would you go back?
Would you?

If you had seen the women bear
Their heavy load with none to share
Had heard them weep with none to care,
Would you go back?
Would you?

If you had seen the glorious sight
When heathen people in their night,
Were brought from darkness into light,
Would you go back?
Would you?

Yet still they wait, a weary throng,
They've waited, some so very long,
When shall despair be turned to song?
I'm going back!
Wouldn't you?

E. Doerksen

Anna's inner struggles about the future were not resolved in one session. Not only did she face the fact of leaving her children, but she too, like Paul in 2 Cor. 11:23, could draw up a long list of the things she'd gone through while serving the Lord — sorrows, separations, struggles, accidents, suspense, repeated sicknesses unto death, physical fears and sacrifices to the point of near hunger. What if the future held more of the same? Or worse? Should she draw back in fear? Or should she simply trust God and bravely claim His promises?

While searching her Bible in the midst of these thoughts, looking for some specific guidance, she came across Philippians chapter one. Suddenly it stood out before her eyes wanting to catch her attention. She read and reread the chapter and then underlined the special verses.

"According to my earnest expectation and hope, that in nothing I shall be ashamed, but that with all boldness as always, so now also Christ shall be magnified in my body, whether it be by life or by death. For to me to live is Christ and to die is gain. Being confident of this very thing that He which hath begun a good work in you (me) will perform it until the day of Jesus Christ" (Phil. 1:20,21,6).

"This is the guidance I've been praying for," she told herself. "Why, I'll make these verses my special motto for the future, the 'desire of my heart' for the new term before me. I'll tuck them away as a constant truth to live by."

The future now presented a challenge. No matter what it might bring, the future had a purpose. The God who had seemed a mystery and held back the answers she longed for, had revealed Himself to her, not once but many times. He was real and He was good. For His sake she would press on, yes, ever press on.

The last farewells at the airport in Winnipeg had been spoken. Anna turned back for one last wave before disappearing down the terminal's gangway to the plane. For at least one thought-filled eyewitness there was a message in her tear-streaked face, her very posture and final gestures. It said," I have a goal, a purpose, a calling to fulfill. Nothing must keep me back."

Paul also had that goal. "I press toward the mark for the prize of the high calling of God in Christ Jesus" (Phil 3:14).